The Philosophy of Nature

The Philosophy of Nature

A Guide to the New Essentialism

Brian Ellis

McGill-Queen's University Press
Montreal & Kingston • Ithaca

B
105
.E65
E44
2002

ISBN 0-7735-2473-8   (hardcover)
ISBN 0-7735-2474-6   (paperback)

Legal deposit second quarter 2002
Bibliothèque nationale du Québec

Published simultaneously outside North America
by Acumen Publishing Limited

McGill-Queen's University Press acknowledges the financial support of
the Government of Canada through the Book Publishing Development
Program (BPIDP) for its activities.

National Library of Canada Cataloguing in Publication Data

Ellis, B. D. (Brian David), 1929-
        The philosophy of nature : a guide to the new essentialism /
Brian Ellis.

Includes bibliographical references and index.
ISBN 0-7735-2473-8 (bound).—ISBN 0-7735-2474-6 (pbk.)

        1. Essence (Philosophy). 2. Necessity (Philosophy).
3. Philosophy of nature. I. Title.

B105.E65E44 2002   111'.1   C2002-901393-3

Designed and typeset by Kate Williams, Abergavenny.
Printed and bound by Biddles Ltd., Guildford and King's Lynn.

Contents

v

Introduction

Essentialism is an ancient theory about the sources of power and order in the world. Its basic thesis is that the laws of nature are immanent in the things that exist in nature, rather than imposed on them from without. Thus, essentialists hold that things behave as they do, not because they are forced or constrained by God, or even by the laws of nature, but, rather, because of the intrinsic causal powers, capacities and propensities of their basic constituents and how they are arranged. The new essentialism is a modern version of this ancient theory. The new essentialists, like the old, insist that the same things, constituted in the same ways, from the same basic components, would have to behave in the same kinds of ways in any other world in which they might exist, for what they do or could do is of their essence. The things that exist are thus supposed to determine what the laws of nature are, rather than the laws determine how things must behave. But the new essentialism, unlike the old, is a metaphysic for a modern scientific understanding of the world.

The essentialist theory of laws of nature stands in contrast to the "divine command" theory and its modern secular counterparts. According to the divine command theory, the laws of nature are imposed on things by God. They are God's commands for the natural world. Descartes and Newton both thought of laws of nature in this way, and both attributed the existence of invariable laws to the coherence and consistency of God's commands. According to this traditional view, material things are bound to act according to the laws of nature, because such things are themselves powerless. Only spiritual beings, such as God, human minds or angels were thought to

1

be capable of acting on their own account. They, and they alone, were thought to have genuine causal powers.

In the eighteenth century, secularized versions of the divine command theory were developed. Instead of thinking of God as the source of all power and order, some natural philosophers of the period began to speak of the "forces of nature" as the source of nature's activity. But, in an important respect, the theory remained unchanged. The things in the world were just as passive as ever, only now they were being pushed or pulled around, willy-nilly, by forces. The philosopher David Hume, who was an atheist, took the further step of eliminating the forces, but he too retained the concept of nature as essentially passive. According to Hume, things do not move as they do because they are caused by anything to do so. They just do so move; and this is a brute fact about the world. Causes are illusions of causal powers in action, he argued, but really there are no such things as causal powers.

The view that things in nature are essentially passive, and obedient to nature's laws, was very widely shared by philosophers of all persuasions in the eighteenth century, as indeed it has been ever since. It was accepted not only by Descartes, Newton and Hume, but also by Locke and Kant, and therefore by the founding fathers of all of the major philosophical traditions of western Europe. Let us call this still-dominant world-view "passivism". Passivism has both religious and secular versions, as we have seen. If the secular versions have tended to dominate scientific thinking about the sources of power and order in the world since the eighteenth century, the religious versions have dominated religious thinking. For the religious, passivism provides a clear role for God as the author of the laws of nature. If the laws of nature are God's commands for an essentially passive world, as they believe, then presumably God also has the power to suspend the laws of nature, and so perform miracles. But belief in passivism does not depend on religious belief, or even on faith in science. It is such an established way of thinking that to many it seems to be plain common sense. Surely, it will be said, the things that do exist in this world could just as well exist in worlds with different laws of nature, for nothing is easier to imagine than this possibility. Therefore, it is argued, the things that do exist in this world cannot be the source of the laws that are specific to this world. The laws must have some other origin.

To be a passivist, one must believe that inanimate things are capable of acting only as directed – depending, for example, on how they are pushed or pulled around by God, or by the forces of nature (or, in Hume's case, by what the laws of nature happen to be). A passivist therefore believes that the tendencies of things to behave as they do can never be inherent in the things themselves. They must always be imposed on them from the outside. The forces of nature, for example, are always seen as being external to the objects on which they act. They act *on* them, or *between* them, but the things themselves are never the source of any activity. Even the so-called "internal" forces that bind things together are thought to be external really, since they are external to the parts on which they act. Hence their internality is only relative.

For an essentialist, however, this is all wrong. Things behave as they do, they say, not because of any external constraints that force them to, but because this is how they are intrinsically disposed to behave in the circumstances. The forces of nature are the kinds of causal influences that things exert on each other, and the things themselves are always the agents of these influences. Thus, if one thing causes another to do something, then this is because it has the causal power to do so, and it achieves its effect by the exercise of this power. It acts, and the other thing reacts. Or, perhaps they interact, so that each responds to the other. Essentialists thus suppose that the inanimate objects of nature are genuine causal agents: things capable of acting or interacting. They do not think of them as just the passive participants in processes that are externally driven or governed, as all passivists must. Inanimate things are not, of course, free agents, as human beings might reasonably be thought to be. But they are agents, nevertheless, in the more primitive sense of being genuine actors on the stage, doing things, and reacting to things.

Moreover, essentialists suppose that when things act or interact with other things, they do so in ways that depend on their intrinsic natures, for the ways in which they act or interact stem from their intrinsic causal powers. Passivists do not believe that inanimate things have any such powers. If they are disposed to behave in one way rather than another in any given circumstances, they say, then this fact must depend on what the laws of nature happen to be, and how they apply in the circumstances. Consequently, they argue, the dispositional properties of things must always depend on external factors – namely, on what the laws or forces of nature are. Therefore, according to passivism, the causal powers of things can never be wholly intrinsic. Essentialists take the opposite view to this. They argue that things must behave in the sorts of ways they do not because the laws of nature require them to, but rather because this is how they are intrinsically disposed to behave. The causal powers, capacities and propensities of things, they say, are genuine properties, which they are bound to display in their various actions and interactions.

Passivism had its origins in medieval philosophy. It became closely associated with mechanism in the seventeenth century and, with the unprecedented success of Newton's *Philosophiae Naturalis Principia Mathematica*, it became the dominant metaphysic of the day, and remained so for the next two centuries while mechanism reigned supreme. In the first decade of the twentieth century, mechanism began to give ground to the emerging theories of relativity and quantum mechanics, but passivism survived these events, and Newtonian mechanistic ways of thinking about the world and the forces of nature, still dominated in philosophical circles. Indeed, they still dominate. There is probably no more deeply entrenched philosophical thesis than that the laws of nature are contingent (i.e. could have been otherwise). But if things are naturally active, and have their most basic causal powers essentially, as essentialists claim, then things would have to act according to their natures in any world in which they might exist, rather than as any imposed laws of nature might require. Consequently, essentialists must reject the deeply entrenched philosophical belief in the contingency of laws. The laws of nature, they say, depend on what kinds of things exist in the world, and hold necessarily of all such things.

Essentialism is not yet widely accepted by philosophers. One has to go all the way back to Aristotle to find a truly notable defender of essentialism. Yet essentialism is precisely the sort of theory that one would expect any modern scientific realist to accept, for a realist would now be hard pressed to make much sense of the passive, and intrinsically inert, world in which the laws of nature are supposed to operate. The world, according to modern science, seems to be not innately passive, but fundamentally active and reactive. It is certainly not a mechanistic world of things having only the attributes of extension and impenetrability, as Descartes's and Locke's worlds were. Rather, it is a dynamic world consisting of more or less transient objects that are constantly interacting with each other, and whose identities appear to depend only on their roles in these causal processes.

I assume that this appearance is also reality. That is, I assume that the identities of things of the most fundamental kinds are wholly dependent on how they are disposed to act. If protons, for example, are such fundamental things, then for anything to be a proton it must always be disposed to behave as protons do, and, conversely, if anything is ever disposed to behave as a proton does, then it is a proton. That is, there are no protons in disguise, and there are no fake or ersatz protons. If this is true, and I think there is good reason to suppose that it is, then protons, or electrons, or any other fundamental particles for that matter, could not behave according to different laws without ceasing to be things of the kind they are. Moreover, nothing else could take their places. If you changed any of the fundamental things that existed in nature, then you would change the world, but the fundamental particles that actually exist could not, logically could not, have causal roles different from the ones they actually have.

It follows that the laws of nature that describe the causal powers of things cannot be contingent – that is, laws that could well have been otherwise. On the contrary, since their causal powers are among their essential properties, they would not be particles or fields of the kinds they are if they were not disposed to behave according to these laws. So the laws cannot be changed. They cannot even be varied. Not even an omnipotent God could change the laws of nature without changing the things on which they are supposed to act. Therefore, the idea that the laws of physics are contingent, and superimposed on intrinsically passive things that have identities that are independent of the laws of their behaviour, is one that lies very uneasily with modern science.

The new essentialism that is now being developed as a metaphysic for modern science is compatible with this intuition. It is not a reversion to Aristotelianism, or an attempt to resuscitate medieval views about the nature of reality. On the contrary, its origins are decidedly twentieth century. Essentialist distinctions between the natural kinds of substances, for example, depend on the existence of quantum discreteness in the world, for it is this discreteness at the quantum level that ultimately guarantees that such distinctions are real and ontologically based – not just distinctions that we have imposed on nature for our own purposes. And this fact turns out to be crucial for the viability of modern essentialism. Aristotle was able to believe in natural kinds (although he did not call them this) because of the diversity, and apparent distinctness, of the various animal and plant species that he knew about. But the idea that biological species are natural kinds has not survived criticism, especially in the light of Darwin's theory of evolution by natural selection. However, the new essentialism is not a defence of Aristotle's theory of *biological* kinds, and does not depend on it. It depends rather on the recognition that there are hierarchies of natural *physical* kinds, formally like the supposed hierarchies of biological species, but real kinds, neverthe-less, existing at a deeper level.

*****

This book is written as an introduction to the new essentialism. It is not a technical book, and it is not intended to engage with the current debates in the philosophical journals. Rather, it is a personal overview of an emerging philosophical position. My aim in writing the book is to make the new essentialism much more widely accessible to readers than it is at present, for it is an exciting position that deserves to be much more widely known and appreciated. It is not a scholarly work that I present, although it is firmly based on scholarship. For those who want a more scholarly account of the new essentialism, I refer them to my recently published *Scientific Essentialism* (Cambridge University Press, 2001). The present book is largely based on this earlier work, but it is new in its conception, and contains new material. In writing it, I have tried to avoid using technical philosophical terms but, where their use has seemed to me to be unavoidable, I have been careful to explain them.

The new essentialism arises from the failure of the metaphysical systems that currently dominate modern philosophy to provide adequate foundations for contemporary theories about the nature of reality, for the dominant metaphysics of the present age are still essentially those of the mechanistic world-view that was introduced by the great philosophers and scientists of the seventeenth and eighteenth centuries. The processes by which things occur in the world may no longer be considered to be mechanistic, certainly not as Newton's theories were, but the metaphysics of nature that underlie much of our thinking about the world are still, nevertheless, much more appropriate to a mechanical world-view than to a modern scientific one, for these metaphysical systems are direct descendants of Hume's great *Treatise of Human Nature*, which was completed in 1736 when the influences of Locke and Newton were at their peak. Hume's theory about the nature of reality thus remains effectively in remote control of much of our thinking about the world, and influences it, often subtly, without our even being aware of it. Consequently, if essentialism were to emerge as the dominant metaphysic of the coming age, then we should expect it to influence our thinking about the world just as profoundly.

Challenges to Humean metaphysics have been gathering strength since the 1970s, and a new essentialist metaphysic that is strongly anti-Humean has at last begun to emerge. For many years essentialism was considered to be beyond the pale in philosophy, a relic of discredited Aristotelianism. But this is no longer so. The revival of essentialism owes much to the work of Saul Kripke (1972) and Hilary Putnam (1975), who made belief in essences or essential natures once more respectable. At about the same time, Rom Harré and Edwin Madden (1975) boldly argued against Hume's theory of causation, and developed an alternative theory based on the assumption that there are genuine causal powers in nature. In the late 1970s and early 1980s, Fred Dretske (1977), Michael Tooley (1977), Chris Swoyer (1982) and David Armstrong (1983) all developed strong alternatives to Hume's theory of the laws of nature, as did John Carroll (1994), and their theories of natural necessity laid the foundations for the later essentialist ones. Sydney Shoemaker (1980, 1983) built on the earlier work of Rom Harré on causal powers to develop a thoroughly non-Humean theory of properties, which is a vital ingredient of the new essentialism. Roy Bhaskar (1978) developed a realist theory of science that foreshadowed some of the later developments in the new essentialism. With the exception of Kripke, and perhaps of Putnam, these philosophers are all distinguished by their realism about the objects, properties and processes described by science. That is, they are all scientific realists. They are also distinguished by their direct and speculative approach to metaphysics, for they consider the programme of logical analysis that has dominated twentieth-century philosophy to be irrelevant to the development of a sound metaphysics of nature. Metaphysics these days is unashamedly speculative.

The new essentialism has evolved from these beginnings, and can now reasonably claim to be a comprehensive philosophy of nature. Many philosophers from around the world, including Sydney Shoemaker, Charles Martin, George Molnar, George Bealer, John Bigelow, Caroline Lierse, Evan Fales, Crawford Elder, Nicholas Maxwell, Nancy Cartwright and John Heil, have contributed in various ways to its development. So the new essentialism is not just a personal view, but an emerging metaphysical perspective that is the culmination of many different attempts to arrive at a satisfactory post-Humean philosophy of nature. Nevertheless, the perspective that I shall present is my own, and I shall not attempt to differentiate it from others, or evaluate the other contributions that have been made to the general programme.

CHAPTER 1

Essentialist Philosophies of Nature

Classical essentialism

Classical essentialism was a theory of nature developed in ancient Greece, mainly by Aristotle (4th century BCE), to provide a meta-physical foundation for the science of that time. It sought to explain and synthesize Greek knowledge in fields as diverse as cosmology and biology. It was the cornerstone of Aristotle's metaphysics. Aristotle believed that the world below the sphere of the moon consists ultimately of four elements (earth, air, fire and water), while the heavens above are composed of a special element (the ether) that is essentially different from any of the others. Each natural kind of object, or substance, he thought, has its own special place in the cosmos, and its own natural motion. Thus, heavenly bodies were supposed naturally to move in circles (or combinations of circles) about the centre of the cosmos, while terrestrial bodies of the various kinds all had their proper places, and would naturally return to these places by the shortest paths should they be forced out of them. There were no forces required to maintain the circular motions of the stars or planets, Aristotle argued, and none were required to bring heavy objects back to earth, once they had been lifted up, for these motions were all natural motions. Forces would only be required to prevent them from occurring, or cause the bodies to move otherwise.

Aristotle believed that the things that exist in the world can all be divided into those that exist by nature, those that exist by art and those that exist by chance. Those that exist by nature, Aristotle supposed, include the animals and their parts, the plants and the elements of which all terrestial and celestial bodies are ultimately composed. The things that exist by nature, Aristotle argued, are distinguished from things of other kinds in that each has *within itself* (Aristotle's emphasis) various principles of change and resistance to change: principles that are the intrinsic causes of its formal development (its formal causes), and of its role in nature (its final cause). These principles, Aristotle argued, are distinctive of the various kinds of things that exist by nature, and are definitive of them. They are their *essences*. The essence of an elephant, for example, is the particular set of principles of growth and development inherent in the semen of the male elephant that sired it, and it is in virtue of its having just these principles (and, of course, this particular father), that it is the elephant it is. (Aristotle thought that the mother mainly had the lesser role of supplying the matter for the embryo's development, but he did allow that she might have some influence on the form.)

In general, Aristotle believed that material objects of various kinds are distinguished from each other by the substances of which they are composed (their material causes), by their shapes, sizes, textures, arrangements of parts and so on (their formal causes), by what brought them into being (their efficient causes), and by the purposes for which they exist (their final causes). The "natural kinds", as we should now call them, are distinguished by being the products of nature, rather than those of art or chance.

According to Aristotle's theory, things of different natural kinds must be essentially different from each other: they must have different intrinsic determinants of their characteristics and development. Aristotle did not, of course, deny that the actual development of a thing that is a member of a natural kind may be affected by poor nutrition, or by other accidental circumstances. But these are extrinsic (efficient) causes, he would have said, acting to counter or modify the natural development that is intrinsically determined. Thus, an animal that is naturally four-legged might lose a leg through accident, but it still remains essentially a four-legged creature, for that is what it is by nature. Aristotle was thus able to solve the ancient (even in his day) problem of identity through change. The acorn and the oak tree are two very different objects. Nevertheless, they may be just different stages of what is essentially one and the same thing.

If things that are members of a given natural kind must be essentially the same – have the same internal dynamic – then we should expect to find that these things have certain distinctive characteristics that are the direct consequences of their essential sameness. The distinctive characteristics will necessarily include those that anything must have if it is to be a member of the kind, or which nothing could lose without ceasing to be a member of it. Aristotle's essentialism thus leads to a very important distinction between *essence* and *accident*. The essence of a thing refers to those characteristics it has by nature, and that it could not lose without becoming denatured – that is, ceasing to be a thing of that nature. The accidental properties of a thing are those it has acquired accidentally, or that depend on its particular circumstances, and that it could lose without loss of identity.

Aristotle's essentialism was developed primarily to explain the existence and continuation through many generations of apparently distinct species of animals and plants, the degree to which these species are evidently adapted to the world about them, the separations of function of the various parts of animals, and the specific design features of these parts. Aristotle believed that these salient facts about the animal and plant kingdoms could be explained if it could reasonably be supposed that each animal and plant has within itself a certain intrinsic capacity for development, which could be passed on in the process of reproduction to the next generation. The concepts of formal and final causation that are postulated to account for this capacity are thus central to Aristotle's account of these matters, and it comes as no surprise to learn that the essence of an animal or plant kind consists of the formal and final causal powers of its soul (human, animal or vegetative). Aristotle can thus be said to have believed in the existence of intrinsic causal powers.

The final cause is said by Aristotle to be "that for the sake of which a thing is (i.e. exists)" (Metaphysics V, 1013a, 33). Final causes are thus essentially *purposive*, and explanations given in such terms are said to be "teleological" (from the Greek word *telos* meaning, roughly, "purpose"). Philosophers and scientists today would generally agree that teleological explanations have no role to play in science. They are relevant to understanding works of art or craft, perhaps, where the artist's or the craftman's intentions are in question. But they are not relevant in such fields as physics or biology, where the objects of study are not artefacts, but things that exist by nature. It is true that we are often interested in the causal roles of things in complex ongoing systems (as we are, for example, in ecology or physiology). That is, the question of how something functions to help maintain the system is raised. But this is not a question of purpose; it is one of functional role, which is different. If something is brought into being in order to fulfil a certain role, then it is brought into being for this purpose. But something might happen to exist that fulfils a certain role, even though it was not brought into being for this purpose. It might just have this role accidentally. Aristotle's *telos* is therefore much more like purpose than it is like functional role, for the *telos* of anything that exists by nature is *never* accidental. Indeed, Aristotle assumes that everything that exists by nature has a *telos* that belongs to its essence. Hence the *telos* of anything that exists by nature exists independently of anything else. He further postulates that the ultimate aim of all philosophical (including scientific) enquiry is to know the *telos* of things: the reasons for their existence. In this sense, the final cause is the highest of all causes.

Modern essentialism

The new essentialism retains the Aristotelian idea that there are natural kinds of substances (roughly, kinds of things of a material nature), but rejects Aristotelian essentialism about animal and plant species. According to the new essentialism, the true natural kinds of substances exist only at a much deeper level than that of living species. They include the basic kinds of physical and chemical substances, such as the various species of atoms, molecules and subatomic particles, but not the biological kinds. The biological species concepts are really *cluster concepts*, a modern essentialist will say. They have some similarities with natural kinds concepts, as we shall see, but the biological species are not natural kinds.

The new essentialism also retains Aristotelian ideas about essential properties, but it distinguishes more clearly than Aristotle ever did between "individual essences" and "kind essences". The individual essence of a thing is the set of its characteristics in virtue of which it is the *individual* it is. This sort of essence is at issue, for example, if we are dealing with questions of personal identity. Is this man now the same man as that man 30 years ago? The kind essence of a thing, on the other hand, is the set of its properties in virtue of which it is a thing of the *kind* it is. Of these two conceptions of essence, the most important one, from the point of view of scientific understanding, is the kind essence, since science is much more concerned with kinds than with individuals. Consequently, when I speak about the essences, or essential properties, of things, I should always be understood as talking about their kind essences unless I specifically indicate otherwise. The essence of a copper atom, for example, will be just the set of its properties in virtue of which it is a copper atom, and which it could not lose without ceasing to be a copper atom. It is not the set of properties in virtue of which it is the particular thing it is.

Aristotle's concept of final cause – that is, that for the sake of which a thing exists – has no role in the new essentialism. The parts of animals do not exist for the sake of the animals of which they are parts, as Aristotle believed, nor organisms for the sake of the ecological systems in which they are found. Nor do modern essentialists conceive of the world as a grand teleological system in which the parts exist for the sake of the whole. However, modern essentialists do believe that things may have potentialities for development, or have inbuilt behavioural dispositions of one kind or another. Indeed, they believe that all things belonging to natural kinds have at least some such dispositional properties. So the modern essentialist's world is not as organismic as Aristotle's world, and it is never true to say that its parts exist for the sake of any greater wholes. But it is an integrated world, nevertheless, in which things are intrinsically disposed to interact with each other in various ways, depending on their essential natures.

Today's essentialists suppose that the basic dispositions of things to interact with each other in the ways in which they do derive from the intrinsic causal powers, capacities and propensities of their most fundamental constituents. They suppose that these causal powers, and the like, are among the essential properties of things of these kinds, and therefore properties that things of these kinds have necessarily, since they could not possibly fail to have them, while yet being things of these kinds. Electrons, for example, are necessarily charged particles. That is, they are necessarily disposed to generate and respond in certain ways to electromagnetic fields. If a particle lacked this causal power, essentialists say, then, whatever else it might be, it would not be an electron. So, there is at least this affinity between the new essentialism and the old. According to the new essentialism (as well as the old), the essential properties of things may include their potentialities: their dispositions to act or react in various ways, depending on their circumstances.

Passivism denies this possibility. If things are essentially passive, as defenders of this view insist, then nothing can be intrinsically disposed to act in any one way rather than any other. Some things, in their special circumstances, might be disposed to behave in some ways rather than others, but only because the laws of nature happen to be as they are, and the things happen to be in the states in which they are.

Change either of these conditions sufficiently, and they would no longer be so disposed. Hence, according to passivism, the dispositional properties of things are *never* determined just by their intrinsic natures.[1] Remember, the laws of nature are not supposed to be immanent in things, as essentialists believe, but externally imposed on them. Remember, too, that material things are supposed to be essentially passive, and so incapable of having any intrinsic dispositions. So, how a thing is disposed to behave can only depend on its passive, non-dispositional properties, and on what the laws of nature happen to be. Any dispositions that material things might have must therefore be wholly dependent on the passive states they are in, and on the laws of nature as they apply to things in those states.

Modern essentialism works with a much stricter conception of natural kinds than the old Aristotelian theory. In Aristotle there is the idea of things existing by nature, and it is evident that Aristotle believed that different individuals could have the same nature, since most of the essences he discusses are the essences of kinds of things, rather than individuals. So he is clearly committed to the existence of natural kinds in something like the modern sense of this term, and to the view that such kinds have distinctive essences. But in Aristotle there is a certain looseness about membership of a natural kind, and properties that are said to be essential to a kind may occasionally not be present. A man may lack rationality, for example, even though rationality is said to be essential to human kind. Modern essentialists would not accept such looseness. They would insist that any two members of the same natural kind must be identical in all essential respects. Moreover, they would insist that the essential properties of a thing be properties or structures in virtue of which it is a thing of the kind it is, and which it could not lack, or lose, while still being a member of the kind. Essentiality implies necessity in the strict sense of metaphysical necessity.

Metaphysical necessity is one of several species of necessity distinguished by essentialists. These species of necessity do not differ

---

1. Remember that, on the standard world-view, the laws of nature are imposed on things from without, as though by the command of God. Therefore, the dispositions to behaviour cannot be essential to the things on which they are imposed. Change the states of things, or change the laws of nature, and you must change their dispositional properties. Therefore, the same things could, in principle, exist in other worlds in which they had different dispositional properties. The dispositional properties of things are therefore not among their essential properties.

from each other in strictness, for none of them allows any possible exception. The other species of necessity that are commonly recognized are *formal logical* necessity and *linguistic* (i.e. *analytic*) necessity. Propositions that are necessary in any of these strict senses are true in all possible worlds. That is, they are such that not even God (even if He should be an omnipotent being) could create a world in which any of them are false. The different kinds of necessities differ from each other in the manner in which they are grounded.

Formal logical necessities are grounded in logical form, that is, in the meanings of the connectives and operators of the language. Thus if a statement is formally logically necessary, then it is true under all interpretations of its non-logical terms. The proposition that horses either exist or do not exist, for example, is formally logically necessary. Substitute any other name for "horses", and you still have a necessarily true proposition. So horses can be interpreted as any kind of thing you like, and this proposition will still be true.

Linguistic or analytic necessities are sentences that are true in virtue of the meanings of words, and these are also true in all possible worlds. But they are not true under all interpretations of their non-logical terms. On the contrary, their truth derives from the conventions of language, and is therefore strongly dependent on how the non-logical terms of the language are understood. The sentence "A bachelor is an unmarried man", for example, is an analytic sentence of English, and this English sentence must be true in any world in which it is significant. Of course, there might be worlds in which there are no men, or where there is no institution of marriage, but it would still be true, vacuously true,[2] even in these worlds, that a bachelor is an unmarried man; it is just that we should have no use for this part of the vocabulary of English in describing such a world.

Metaphysical necessities are propositions that are true in virtue of the essences of things. Of course, if one does not believe that there are any natural kinds, or if one does not accept that things have essential natures, then one will not believe that there are any metaphysical necessities. But for an essentialist the concept of metaphysical necessity is fundamental. To explicate the concept of metaphysical neces-

---

2. In logic, a general proposition is said to be "vacuously true", or true by default, if it is about an empty class of things. For example, the proposition "All griffins like chocolate" would be said to be true just because the class of griffins is empty. The reasons for adopting this convention need not concern us here. They are mainly reasons of systemic simplicity. See any logic textbook for a detailed explanation.

sity, essentialists distinguish between "real essences" and "nominal essences". The real essence of a thing of a given kind is that set of its properties or structures in virtue of which it *is* a thing of that kind. The nominal essence of a thing of a given kind is that set of its properties or structures in virtue of which it *is described as* a thing of that kind. The two concepts, although formally similar, are really quite different. The nominal essence of a thing depends on what distinctions we care to make, and how we choose to make them. It thus refers to how we classify things in the world, and to the language we use to mark the different classes. But the real essence of a thing of a given kind is independent of our conceptualization of reality, and also of the language we use to describe it, for the real essences of things refer to their natural classifications, and these have to be discovered by scientific investigation.

Consider the proposition that water is H_2O. The fact that water is essentially a compound of hydrogen and oxygen was discovered in the eighteenth century, and its molecular formula was worked out in the nineteenth. But these are not the facts on the basis of which the distinction between water and other substances initially depended, and water would still be H_2O even if these facts had never been discovered. So the proposition that water is H_2O is not analytic: it is not simply true in virtue of the conventions of language. It is, in fact, true independently of these conventions, since its truth is independent of whether anyone has the language to express it. Moreover, if it is true, then it is necessarily true, for the molecular structure of water is essential to its nature. The substance in the glass in front of me would not be water if it were not H_2O, however like water it may be in appearance, savour, function, and so on. Hilary Putnam (1975) tells the story of an imaginary place called Twin Earth on which there is a race of beings who are very like people, who speak a language that is very like English. But the lakes, seas and reservoirs of Twin Earth are filled with a substance that they call "water", which functions just like water does for us on Earth, but which has a different molecular structure, XYZ. Putnam argues, correctly in the view of modern essentialists, that, however like water this stuff may be in appearance and function to the stuff that we call "water", it is not water. The word "water" in Twin Earth English refers to something other than water. Nothing hinges on what we call "water" here, or what Twin Earthians call "water" there. It is clear that there are two quite distinct kinds of stuff: H_2O and XYZ. It is also clear that, if the stuff on Earth is in fact H_2O, then it is so necessarily. It does not matter what it is called: *that* stuff is H_2O. And, if we have the science right, then it is necessarily H_2O.

The concept of metaphysical necessity employed here is fundamental to modern essentialism, and I shall have more to say about it later. For now, it is sufficient to note its two most important properties. First, a metaphysical necessity is a genuine necessity. If something is metaphysically necessary, then it must be the case, and there is no possible state of affairs in which it would not be. Not even God, if there were such a being, could create a world in which anything that is metaphysically necessary is false. If water is H_2O, and this is its essential nature, then not even God could create a world in which water is not H_2O. God might conceivably create a world in which some substance other than water has a functionally similar role to the one that water has on Earth. But, as the Twin Earth example illustrates, this stuff is not water. The inhabitants of Twin Earth just call it "water".

Secondly, metaphysical necessities have to be discovered by scientific investigation. They are not discoverable, as other necessities are, just by considering meanings. On the contrary, they depend on what there is in the world, and how the world is structured. In philosophers' jargon, metaphysical necessities are a posteriori.[3] Logical and linguistic necessities, on the other hand, are a priori. That is, they can be discovered, without investigating their subject matter. To show that a sentence expresses an analytic truth, or a formal logical truth, we need only reflect on the meanings of terms, connectives and operators of the language. To show that a bachelor is an unmarried

---

3. The terms "a priori" and "a posteriori" are terms of art in philosophy. Literally, "a priori" means "before the event", and "a posteriori" means "after the event". However, when used in philosophy, they mean, roughly, "independently of experience" and "in the light of experience", respectively. These terms were used by Kant to distinguish two kinds of knowledge. Thus, "a priori knowledge" refers to what can be known independently of experience, and "a posteriori knowledge" to knowledge that depends on experience. Kant said, for example, that we can know a priori that $2 + 2 = 4$, or that two straight lines can never enclose a space. The term "a priori" was thus used to refer to what was thought to be prior in the order of knowledge. Once we understand the meanings of the words involved in these sentences, he said, then we know, or at least we can prove, that they must be true. A posteriori knowledge, on the other hand, is knowledge that we can gain only through experience. It is not given, as an axiom or definition might be supposed to be given. Nor is it derivable from anything that is given in this way. Hume made a similar distinction between what he called "matters of fact" and "relations of ideas". Matters of fact are a posteriori, and so depend on experience. Relations of ideas are a priori, and are independent of experience.

man, for example, we do not have to investigate bachelors. Indeed, if we did not already know that bachelors are unmarried men, we could not even begin such an investigation. However, to show that a proposition expresses a metaphysical necessity, it is not enough to sit and reflect on the language in which it is stated. It has to be shown that it is true in virtue of the properties that it attributes to things, and, moreover, that these are among the essential properties of these things.

If metaphysical necessities are discoverable only by empirical investigation, then the same must be true of metaphysical possibilities, for, in general, what is possible is just what is not necessarily not the case. The concepts of necessity and possibility are thus correlative.[4] However, philosophers tend to be a bit casual about the so-called logical possibilities, and many of them subscribe to the view that if something is readily imaginable, and we can see no obvious contradiction, formal or otherwise, in its being the case, then it is logically possible. No other considerations are thought to be relevant. But if essentialists are right, then these sorts of considerations do not establish logical possibility. For anything to be logically possible it must also be metaphysically possible. That is, it must be compatible with the essential natures of the things involved.

Most philosophers believe that the so-called "logical modalities" – that is, logical necessities and possibilities – are knowable a priori, and that if anything is readily conceivable, and (apparently) free from contradiction, then this is enough to establish that it is at least logically possible. It might not be physically possible, or technically possible. But these concepts of possibility are held to be more restrictive than that of mere logical possibility. If essentialists are right, then these a priori considerations do not establish logical possibility, for it also has to be shown that what is being envisaged is

---

4. Philosophers consequently make parallel distinctions between kinds of necessities and possibilities. Logical necessities go with logical possibilities, metaphysical necessities with metaphysical possibilities, and so on. The strictest kind of necessity is usually called "logical necessity" and, therefore, the least restrictive kind of possibility is called "logical possibility". However, these terms can be misleading, since to call anything "logically necessary" is to suggest that it is a truth of logic, and consequently, that what is "logically possible" is just what is not contrary to any truth of logic. Essentialists deny these implications. Metaphysical necessities are no less strict than formal logical necessities; they are just grounded in a different way. Metaphysical necessities are grounded in the natures of things; formal logical necessities are grounded in the structures of the languages we use to talk about them.

metaphysically possible – that is, consistent with the natures of things. For example, we can easily conceive of a substance with a chemical composition other than H_2O (XYZ, say) that behaves physically and chemically just like water, and so is capable of doing duty for water on Twin Earth. Moreover, we can imagine, as Daniel Dennett does, a human being being transported to Twin Earth,[5] and perhaps drinking the "water" there, and speaking to the locals. But an essentialist must doubt whether any of this story describes a logical possibility. Could there really be such a substance in this or any other world that we could visit, or in which beings made of the same stuff as us could exist? Is imaginability enough to establish logical possibility? If not, then the fact that we can easily imagine it does not establish what Dennett needs for his example. The new essentialism must therefore bring with it a new, more realistic, and more down to earth, style of philosophy, which stays much closer to the world as we know it.

---

5. Daniel Dennett imagines this in Dennett (1995: 409). Consider also Dennett's remark on the same page: "this is philosophy, and you can make up whatever details you need to make your thought experiment 'work'". An essentialist would say that you first have to show that the scenario you have imagined is metaphysically possible. The fact that you are able to imagine it does not establish its genuine possibility.

CHAPTER 2

Empiricist and Realist Perspectives on the World

Introduction

My motivation for breaking with the long tradition of Anglo-American philosophy to become an essentialist derives from reflection on the aims of scientific theorizing. The French philosopher Pierre Duhem, writing in 1905, said that there are two principal views about this. According to one – that favoured by Duhem – science aims only to "summarise and classify logically" the laws discovered by observation and experiment, to represent them mathematically, to postulate general principles that can usefully systematize our knowledge in the relevant field, and develop a theoretical structure within which the experimental laws can be derived as special cases. It does not aim to explain the phenomena, he said, or to discover the nature of the reality that gives rise to them. The other view is that science seeks to dig beneath the surface to discover and expose the underlying causes of things, and so reveal a deeper reality. On this view, science seeks not merely to represent things, but also to explain them, where explaining is here understood to be a matter of "strip[ping] reality of appearances covering it like a veil, in order to see the bare reality itself" (Duhem 1954: 7). If a scientist seeks to explain anything in this full-blooded sense, Duhem argued, then he is going beyond his brief as a scientist, and engaging in metaphysics.

Duhem's view was widely shared by philosophers and scientists in the first half of the twentieth century. Science, it was said, should stick to the observed facts, and to what can legitimately be inferred by rational arguments based on those facts. Anything more is speculative or metaphysical, and cannot claim the status of scientific knowledge. This is the philosophical position known as "empiricism".

Empiricism has a long tradition, going back to classical Greek times. In the modern era, the greatest exponents of this position were the seventeenth- and eighteenth-century British empiricists John Locke, George Berkeley and David Hume. Empiricist philosophers have often differed from each other on what they thought could be directly known by observation. Berkeley argued that such knowledge is limited to what we can know most directly by experience, and thus to knowledge of our own sense impressions. But such knowledge, he said, does not tell us how the world really is, independently of its being perceived, or even whether there is such a world. Others allowed some more objective observational judgements to count as being known directly by experience, but questioned whether anything much could be known by inference from such judgements. Hume, for example, argued that inductive inferences are, in principle, unjustifiable and, consequently, that no one can ever properly claim to know that anything is true in general. Nor can they ever claim to have justified belief in what will happen in the future, or in what is happening at other times or places, which are not being observed by anyone. Thus, if Hume is right, the only facts that we can ever really know are particular facts about things that are currently being observed – which, of course, is not good news for science.

By the end of the nineteenth century, empiricists had begun to have a more relaxed view about what is really knowable, although they were still reluctant to believe in the atoms and molecules of chemical theory, or the electromagnetic waves of the theories of light, radiant heat and electrodynamics, because the theories within which these entities were postulated all went considerably beyond what could be justified by observation or experiment, or legitimately inferred by any known rules of inference from the results of such observations. The postulated mechanisms were suspected of being just more or less useful models for representing the phenomena to be explained, rather than the mechanisms that actually produced them. Pierre Duhem, and other influential philosophers of the period, shared these doubts.

Ernst Mach, the founder of modern positivism, accepted empiricist arguments about the limits of human knowledge, and added a few twists of his own. First, he was careful always to distinguish what is factual from what is conventional. Science, as he understood it, is a structure of definitions and linguistic conventions overlaid on a basis of observed facts about the world. But the facts and the conventions are not always clearly marked, and often we lose sight of what is factual and what is not. Assumptions are made and accepted as established facts, even though their acceptance has no empirical justification. Mach argued that we have to be clear about what is established as factual, and what is not, if we want to understand what science has achieved, and what has yet to be determined. A great deal of Mach's most important philosophical work is concerned with this distinction. It is said that Mach's philosophical enquiries inspired Einstein to question whether time in any one system is the same as time in any other, and so led him to the seminal idea that time might be relative to a frame of reference. Secondly, Mach argued that anything that has no foundation in linguistic conventions, and is not a hypothesis that might conceivably be tested empirically, is as nothing from the point of view of science. It might have some emotive meaning, or be suggestive of ideas, but it lacks empirical significance and scientific relevance. These were both to become standard positivist theses.

In the years following Mach, positivism and empiricism became widely known as "logical positivism", or "logical empiricism". The adjective "logical" does not signify a significantly new movement, however: it serves only to mark the convergence that occurred in the 1920s between positivism and empiricism, on the one hand, and what was, by then, the dominant philosophical programme – that of logical analysis. Duhem's position was also called "instrumentalism" by many philosophers, because of the instrumental role it assigned to scientific theories. The positivists, like the earlier empiricists, argued that science has no business speculating about the underlying causes of things; they should just get on with the metaphysically neutral job of representing and systematizing our empirical knowledge. They accepted that scientists may sometimes need to construct models of reality as aids in their enquiries. But these models, they said, should be understood precisely for what they are – as more or less useful mental constructs. They are not postulates, they thought, about what we may naively think to be the underlying causes of things. They are just props that we can ultimately remove when the theoretical structure becomes strong enough to bear the weight.

The perspective of scientific realism

My own view is now strongly opposed to the empiricist and positivist traditions. For the most part, I think that science really is in the business of stripping reality of appearances in order to discover the hidden causes of things, and that science has, in fact, successfully revealed a great deal about the underlying structure of reality. This is the common-sense position known as "scientific realism". I was not always a scientific realist, however. As a student in the early 1950s, and as a lecturer in the history and philosophy of science at the University of Melbourne in the late 1950s and early 1960s, I was a positivist, and pursued Mach's programme of trying to sort the factual from the conventional in science. In pursuit of this programme, I worked in the areas of Newtonian dynamics, space-time physics and measurement theory, where Mach's problems seemed to be most pressing. In these areas, the Duhemian view of science seemed to me quite plausible, and I had few reasons then to question Mach's basic outlook.

I now see, though, that these areas are rather special. The theoretical entities of Newtonian dynamics are forces, point masses, instantaneous velocities, and so on, none of which is plausibly an object that is revealed to us by "stripping reality of appearances". In particular, Newton's gravitational forces were always highly suspect entities: weird disembodied causes of motion that are somehow transmitted instantaneously across empty space. Even Newton did not believe in them. So it was easy for me to take the Duhemian view that Newtonian dynamics is just a means of systematizing and representing our knowledge of motion – a process that does not claim to describe the underlying reality. About the causes of gravity, Newton said, he would "make no hypotheses". The theories of space-time physics are likewise just abstract theoretical structures that are plausibly no more than ways of representing and organizing logically the more sophisticated knowledge that we now have about how bodies move. And as for measurement theory, this would seem to have almost nothing to do with the underlying causes of things, for measurement is just the process of assigning numbers to things to represent their various quantitative properties – no doubt a precondition for representing our knowledge of such properties – but hardly a revelation of hidden realities.

The essentialist theory that I now accept derives mainly from taking scientific theories about the underlying causes of things much more seriously, and refocusing on areas of science where such theories abound – particularly chemistry. Our theories of chemical interaction are all causal process theories of precisely the sort that were said by Duhem to be metaphysical, and were therefore said to involve considerations other than those that are proper to science, for these theories were all attempts to describe the underlying causal processes involved in these interactions. They are not abstract model theories like, for example, those that are commonly found in space-time physics. In relativity theory and Newtonian mechanics, the Duhemian account seems to be not too far from the truth, for the aim of physics in these areas is, very plausibly, just to provide a framework for representing objects in space and time, systematic ways of deriving the laws of motion for such objects, and ways of making predictions based on these laws. However, the chemical theories are not even plausibly describable as abstract model theories, as the dynamics of Newton and Einstein were, because nearly everyone who accepts them believes that the theoretical entities of these theories – the atoms and molecules – all exist, really have the properties ascribed to them, and actually take part in interactive processes like those described.

If we were to suppose that these objects and processes were all fictitious, then we should be at a loss to explain how the explanations in which they feature could possibly be so useful, for it would be astounding if theories with fictitious entities were able to account for anything beyond what they were developed to do. Yet, in practice, the theoretical entities of chemistry – the atoms, molecules, molecular structures, electron shell structures, and so on – all feature in many different explanations, and it seems that we are learning more and more about them in the process of studying them. The physicist James Clerk Maxwell once claimed that the mark of the real is that it manifests itself in more than one way. This is right, I think. If you can see something, but cannot feel it, then perhaps it is just an illusion. But if you can see it, and feel it, and weigh it on a beam balance, then it is not an illusion. Atoms, molecules, molecular structures and the like all behave like this. Each postulated entity features in many different scientific explanations, in a number of different areas, just as we should expect if it were a real thing. Moreover, each has been found to have properties that it had not at first been thought to have. If the theoretical entities of chemistry were just useful fictions, as some latter-day empiricists would have us believe, their extraordinary and continuing usefulness would be very hard to explain, for there is no doubt that they behave just *as if* they were real things. And, as my old teacher Jack Smart once remarked, "If the world behaves *as if* things of such and such a kind exist, then the best explanation of this fact is that they really do exist."

The natural kinds structure of reality

Refocusing on chemistry quickly changed my mind about a number of things. First, it made the case for realism, at least in this area, irresistible. It did not convince me that all theories should be understood realistically. I still do not believe that. But I thought the case for realism about the theoretical entities of chemistry was very strong. Secondly, it convinced me that the material world is fundamentally structured into natural kinds, for, on close examination, the chemical elements and compounds all turn out to be natural kinds according to some very strict criteria:

1. The differences between the elements and their various compounds are all real and absolute. They are real because each difference manifests itself in many different ways, and they are absolute because the distinctions are not relative to anyone's epistemic perspective. That is, questions of chemical identity are *never* dependent on our interests, psychologies, perceptual apparatus, languages, practices or choices.

2. The elements and their various compounds are all *categorically distinct* from each other. They are distinct in the sense that there is never a gradual transition from any one chemical kind to any other chemical kind. Consequently, it is never an irresolvable issue to which chemical kind a given chemical substance belongs. Either it has the essential characteristics of the substance, or it lacks them. Where there are such transitions in nature, as there are between the colours, for example, we have to draw a line somewhere if we wish to make a distinction. But in chemistry we never have to do this. The distinctions that exist between the elements and between their various compounds are nature's distinctions, not ours.

3. The distinctions between the chemical kinds are based entirely on *intrinsic* (internal) differences: the chemical substances do not differ only *extrinsically* (i.e. externally) from each other. They may differ in appearance, location or ownership, for example, but their identities as chemical substances never depend on such *extrinsic* (external) factors as these. They depend entirely on their internal constitutions.

4. The chemical elements and compounds all belong in hierarchies. At the lowest level, we have the isotopes of the various elements. These isotopes are species of the atoms of which they are

isotopes. The atoms, in turn, are all capable of being components of molecules, ranging from simple monatomic molecules to highly complex structures involving many thousands of atoms. Each different molecule identifies a different chemical kind.

5. The chemical elements and compounds all have "essential properties": intrinsic properties or structures in virtue of which they are the elements or compounds they are. In most cases, moreover, we now know what these essential properties and structures are. They are their atomic–molecular structures.

There are some very important consequences of this natural kinds structure in chemistry. The existence of the structure implies that there is a very large number of language-independent facts, since each substance, of each kind, necessarily has the properties essential to substances of that kind, and each chemical process necessarily has the dynamical structure of all chemical processes of that kind. Moreover, all of this structure exists independently of human knowledge or language (by criteria 1 and 2). Therefore, at the level of chemistry, it guarantees that there is, objectively, a way that the world is. The aim of chemical science can therefore be seen as being just to discover and describe this objective reality. Further, what is true at the level of chemistry appears also to be true at all deeper levels, for there are evidently natural kinds structures all the way down to the most fundamental kinds of things that we know about. Therefore, it is at least plausible to argue that the primary aim of physical theory generally is not what Duhem said it was, but just the opposite: to discover and lay bare the underlying causes of physical phenomena.

Fixed and variable natural kinds

At higher levels of complexity than the molecular, it is often problematic whether something is or is not a member of a natural kind. Crystals of the same form of the same chemical substance are certainly members of a natural kind, according to the criteria we are using. The same is true of, say, the various solutions of salt in water. But there is a notable difference between these kinds and the elementary ones whose members are individual atoms, molecules or subatomic particles. At the atomic and subatomic levels, things of the same natural kind must always behave (with the same probabilities) in the same ways, since their only intrinsic properties and structures are their essential ones. Electrons, for example, all have precisely the same intrinsic properties. Moreover, they have all of these properties essentially, for they are not properties that can be lost or varied in any way. Consequently, any electron may be substituted for any other electron in any process in which electrons are involved. They are all intrinsically identical. The same is true of copper atoms (of the same isotope). All such atoms have the same nuclear and electronic structure, and are therefore intrinsically the same. Consequently, any copper atom may replace any other copper atom in any process in which copper atoms are involved. At these levels, the members of the natural kinds are, in themselves, identical, and must behave in precisely the same ways. Let us call natural kinds like these that allow no intrinsic variability "fixed natural kinds".

Fixed natural kinds may be contrasted with natural kinds that permit intrinsic variability, that is, natural kinds whose members have causal powers or capacities that are capable of being modified. Let us call these "variable natural kinds". Variable natural kinds exist only at higher levels of organization than the atomic or subatomic. One cannot change the properties of an individual electron, for example, without destroying it – that is, making it something other than an electron. And one cannot teach an individual copper atom any new tricks. But natural kind aggregates, such as crystals of copper sulphate, or pieces of metallic copper, are also members of natural kinds, by my criteria. And these aggregate natural kinds are intrinsically variable in some ways, no doubt due to the variability of the states of aggregation. Crystals, for example, may become electrically charged, and so acquire causal powers they did not have before, and pieces of copper may become stressed, and so lose some of their resilience. The causal powers or capacities of such aggregate kinds are thus variable. Members of the same aggregate natural kind must, of course, all have the essential properties of the kind. Lumps of metallic copper must all have the essential properties of copper. However, as aggregates, they may also have some causal powers, or other dispositional properties, accidentally. Thus aggregate kinds are generally variable natural kinds.

Biological kinds

If there are any biological natural kinds, they would at least have to be variable kinds, for all plants and animals have variable causal powers and capacities. They learn and adapt, and their causal powers wax and wane. So they cannot be assimilated to the natural kinds of chemistry or particle physics whose powers are determined by their intrinsic natures. Nevertheless, there are many good reasons to believe that the biological species are not natural kinds, even though there would appear to be natural distinctions between them that suggest they are. Specifically, they fail the categorical distinctness test (criterion 2), and they lack any distinctive real essences (criterion 5).

Biological species fail the categorical distinctness test for two reasons. First, the distinctions between the extant species are not always clear, and there are some well known cases of continuous variation between what would generally be agreed to be different species. Secondly, and more decisively, the distinctions between current species and their nearest ancestors can never be entirely clear. Consequently, if distinctions have to be made, they must always be made arbitrarily, or in relative ignorance of the past. To illustrate, the distinction between the African elephant and the Indian elephant seems clear enough. Nevertheless, neither species is a natural kind, for we must not forget the ancestral creatures from which they both evolved, or their respective ancestral types. Accepting Darwin's theory of natural selection (which I do), we must suppose that there is a spectrum of elephant-like creatures, stretching back from the present African elephant to some common ancestor with the Indian elephant, and then forward again to the present Indian elephant. Consequently, to achieve a classificatory system that is valid for past times as well as present, we must decide on how to divide this spectrum. Which ancestors of the African elephant will count as African elephants, and which not? Which predecessors of the Indian elephant will be genuine Indian elephants? However, if we have to make such decisions, then the distinctions become *our* distinctions, not nature's. Therefore, if the Darwinian assumption is right, the distinctions between the present-day African and Indian elephants and their nearest ancestral relatives are not already there in the fossil records (or anywhere else) for us to discover. So present species are not natural kinds, even though they are often clearly distinct from one another.

The lack of distinctive real essences for biological species is not so easy to demonstrate, since we do not have ready access to the intrinsic natures of things, and very little access to the intrinsic natures of members of extinct species. However, the overwhelming biological evidence is that the intrinsic natures of animals and plants – that is, their genetic constitutions – show exactly the same variability as the animals and plants do themselves. Animals of the same species have similar genetic constitutions, and those of different species different ones. But the genetic constitutions of organisms are rarely, if ever, the same, *even within the same species*. The problem of trying to define species by their genetic constitutions is therefore similar to that of attempting to define them by their manifest (phenotypical) properties. Neither is capable of a non-arbitrary solution. Moreover, the difficulty of the task is increased once ancestral species are included. If Darwin's theory of natural selection is right, as it surely is, then the same sorts of problems of indeterminacy must arise concerning the status of ancestral species. If we wanted to know which ancestors of the Indian elephant should be considered to be members of the current species, it would not help us to know what their genetic constitutions were. Within the historical record, there are no natural distinctions between genotypes that could serve as a basis for species classifications.

Nevertheless, it may be useful to define a limit concept of "genidentity". Two organisms are genidentical, we may say, if and only if they have exactly the same genetic make-ups. This concept is useful, perhaps, because it enables us to see most clearly the connection between the deep natural kinds structure of reality, and the quasi-natural kinds structure of the biological world, for it is easy enough to prove that every class of genidentical organisms is a natural kind class. The species are not themselves natural kinds, as we have seen, but their genidentical subspecies certainly are – in the very strict sense of the term that is applicable to the variable natural kinds of chemistry. They satisfy all of the criteria for natural kind-hood. It is irrelevant to my purposes how often, or even whether, the relationship of genidentity is instantiated between pairs of organisms. Identical twins, I am told, are rarely genidentical. Perhaps some clones are genidentical; and maybe parthenogenetic guppies are genidentical with their mothers. It matters little. It may well be that every organism is *sui generis*: genidentical only with itself.

Kinds of genidentical organisms could, somewhat eccentrically, be regarded as subspecies of ordinary species. But they are not species as we ordinarily understand this term, since no one such "species" could possibly contain both males and females. Let us call them "microspecies". Then these microspecies are the only genuine natural kinds in the domain of living organisms. The distinctions between them are all clear and sharp, as distinctions between natural kinds must be, and they are all grounded in their different genetic constitutions, which makes them essentially different from each other. Ordinary species, on the other hand, are not natural kinds. Rather, they are clusters of genetically similar microspecies, and, as such, are not sharply distinguishable from their genetically similar ancestors. It is like the divisions along the colour spectrum. Let us suppose, by way of simplification, that the radiation spectrum of light is the essence of its colour. Then the microspecies of colour will be all those kinds of light distinguished by having exactly the same radiation spectra. These kinds of light will all be species of coloured light, and the distinctions between them will all be clear and absolute. But the distinctions between the colours themselves (blue and green, for example) will be as fuzzy as ever, and obviously dependent on our capacities for colour discrimination, and on what we find salient or interesting. So the colours will not be natural kinds, even though their microspecies are. The same is true with animal and plant species. The microspecies of the various kinds of animals and plants are all the natural kinds of genidentical organisms. But the gross species that we distinguish by name are not themselves natural kinds. They are all natural kind clusters.

As human beings, we are members of a natural kind cluster. But most of us are *sui generis* within that cluster. That is, we belong to a microspecies of the cluster defined by our own unique genetic constitutions, and have only ourselves as members. The genidentical species to which we belong are certainly variable natural kinds, since our causal powers and capacities are not fixed by our genetic constitutions. We are able to adapt to new circumstances, learn new ways of behaving, and so on. But our causal powers are not only variable, they are deliberately modifiable. That is, we can deliberately take steps to increase our causal powers in some respects, change our attitudes, revise our priorities, and so on. So human beings, and no doubt some other creatures, not only have variable causal powers, they have deliberately variable ones. But if we, as human beings, have deliberately variable causal powers, then we must have a power of deliberation, which may well be described as a "meta-causal power", since it is essentially a power to change our causal powers. Presumably, this is what our sense of freedom of choice and action comes down to in the end. Fixed agents, like atoms and molecules, have fixed causal powers. Variable agents, like lumps of copper, have variable causal powers, because they can become charged or fatigued. Free agents, such as ourselves, have meta-causal powers.

31

As we move to yet more complex systems, from biological organisms up to ecological or social systems, natural kinds analyses become much less interesting. There are no natural kinds that satisfy the strict criteria applicable to chemical kinds that can readily be distinguished, and there are no sets of intrinsic characteristics of ecological, economic, social or other high-level systems that could plausibly be used to define appropriate microspecies (as genetic make-ups might be used to define biological microspecies). Therefore, however successful the sciences of ecology, economics, sociology and the like might be in achieving their aims, we have no good reason to be realistic about the theoretical entities they employ, for these theoretical entities are invariably just the elements of model theories, precisely like those described by Duhem, and constructed for similar purposes. We should not, for example, be tempted to believe that there are pure market economies, characterized by perfect competition among ideally rational agents, all committed to maximizing their personal utility functions, for that is just economic fantasy. The aim of economic theory is not, realistically, to reveal the essential nature of market economies. It is, or ought rather to be, to construct theoretical models that will enable us to represent and organize logically the statistical laws of economic behaviour that are found to hold in the society with which we are concerned, and provide a theoretical framework for the rational discussion and moral evaluation of alternative economic strategies. Therefore, I would argue, Duhem was right about the social sciences, but wrong about the physical and chemical ones.

The dynamical structure of the world

The natural kinds structure of the world is reflected in the kinds of events and processes that can occur. Each natural kind of thing has its own specific ways of behaving, and also of interacting with other things. Things of the same natural kind have the same essential properties and structures, and so must act, and interact with things of other natural kinds, in basically the same kinds of ways. Things of different natural kinds must have some different ways of behaving, because they have some different essential properties or structures. This being the case, there must be strong restrictions on the kinds of events or processes that can occur in our world. That is, the world must have a dynamic as well as a substantive structure. As before, we may illustrate this thesis by reference to chemistry.

On reflection, it becomes evident that the various kinds of chemical processes that result from causal interactions between chemical substances are themselves all natural kinds, for they all satisfy all of the criteria for natural kind-hood. The chemical processes are all categorically distinct kinds of processes, and the differences between them are real and absolute. The identities of these processes depend only on their intrinsic natures, and the substances involved in them, not on how they are related to anything external. The chemical interactions that do occur in nature, or can be made to occur in laboratories, all belong in hierarchies. Some are oxidations, others reductions. Some are solutions in sulphuric acid, others in nitric acid. Some of these kinds of processes are more general than others, and some include others as species. So just as the chemical elements and compounds exist in hierarchies, so do the chemical processes. Furthermore, each natural kind of chemical process has its own essential nature, namely, a structure that distinguishes it from all other kinds of processes, and in virtue of which it is a process of the kind it is. This is usually indicated by the chemical equation that is used to describe the reaction. So by all of our established criteria, the chemical processes are all members of natural kinds.

What is true at the atomic and molecular levels also appears to be true at all deeper levels. If the chemical events and processes have a natural kinds structure, so, it seems, do the underlying physical events and processes. For example, the subatomic events that produce the optical spectra of the various elements all appear to belong to natural kinds. Each different kind of emission is due to a different kind of energy transformation occurring within the orbital electron structure of the atom, and is categorically distinct from every other kind of emission from this or any other kind of atom. Moreover, these kinds of events also belong in hierarchies, and are to be explained by the corresponding hierarchies of the energy transformation processes that produce them. The Balmer series, for example, is produced by one general kind of energy transformation process occurring in the electron shell structure of the hydrogen atom. The Lyman and Paschen series (in the hydrogen spectrum) are produced by other kinds of energy transformation processes occurring in this structure. Each of these kinds of events or processes has its own essential nature. What makes an emission of light of a particular frequency from a particular sample of hydrogen an instance of a Balmer series emission is its being produced by an energy transformation process of the right kind. If it is not produced in this way, then it is not a Balmer series emission, even if its frequency happens to be identical with a Balmer series frequency.

When we get down to the actions and interactions of the fundamental particles, we find that these too all seem to belong to natural kinds. The decay of a neutron seems to be a natural kind of process. It is quite distinct from any other kind of process that we know about, it has an essential nature, and it is just one of many kinds of natural decay processes. Likewise, β-emission would appear to be a natural kind of radioactive decay process. It has its own specific nature, and it is categorically distinct from other known kinds of radioactive decay processes, such as α-emission and γ-emission. Electron–positron annihilation would also seem to be a natural kind of process. It has its own special nature, and is a species of matter–antimatter interaction. Electromagnetic radiation is also, presumably, a natural kind of process. It is categorically distinct from any other kind of process, as far as we know, and has its own essential nature.

For all of these reasons, it is plausible to suppose that all of the events and processes that can occur in the world are instances of natural kinds. The dynamic structure of the world thus appears to mirror its substantive structure, for both would seem to be natural kinds structures. Indeed, if the world does not have such a structure at the deepest levels – and I am not in a position to say whether it does or not – it would seem to be inexplicable that such a structure should be so evident at the molecular, atomic and subatomic levels that we are currently able to investigate. Modern essentialists assume that this is the way that the world really is. It is, both substantively and dynamically, a natural kinds structure.

Two consequences of the natural kinds structure

The basic natural kinds structure of the world has a number of important implications. Here are two of them. First, there is a long tradition in both Anglo-American and continental European philosophy of denying the existence of objective facts, and consequently of accepting some form of relativism, or anti-realism. Postmodernism, social constructivism and internal realism are three such movements. These movements all stem from the belief that the only reality that we are capable of grasping is one that is filtered through language. Consequently, while there may be a way that the world is *for us*, given the language we speak, there can be no way that it is *absolutely*. There may be a personal, a social, or even a human, perspective on reality, but there can be no truly objective viewpoint. That is, there can be no such thing as "the view from nowhere", as Thomas Nagel expressed it. The reasoning that leads to such conclusions derives from the supposition that our knowledge of the world is all dependent ultimately on how we choose to carve it up into objects and kinds, and thus use words to classify and describe things. Consequently, it is argued, the way that the world is *for us* must be a function of the language we use. However, anyone who accepts that there is a natural kinds structure of the world must reject all of these positions, for, if the natural kinds structure exists, and things belonging to natural kinds have the properties they have necessarily, then there is a network of objective facts existing independently of human language, thought and understanding. Moreover, if we are capable of knowing these facts, as every essentialist must suppose, then all of these subjective or relativist conceptions of reality must be rejected.

Secondly, the existence of a hierarchy of natural kinds of events and processes entails the existence of a corresponding hierarchy of laws of nature. Traditionally, the laws of nature have been considered to be either impositions on nature, as if by the command of God (Descartes, Newton), or else just brute facts about the world that have no deeper explanation (Hume and his followers). However, the postulate of a natural kinds structure of the world enables us to dig a bit deeper, for each natural kind of thing must have its own distinctive ways of behaving, since it is essentially different from everything else, and, if it has any structure at all, then it must have its own distinctive structure too. Thus there will be some quite specific ways in which things of the most specific kinds will naturally be disposed to behave, due to their distinctive essential properties, and there will be other less specific ways of behaving that are common to things belonging to more general kinds. Chlorine, for example, has some quite specific properties and structures that distinguish it from all of the other halogens, and the halogens in turn all have certain distinctive properties and structures that mark them out as kinds of substances different from all other kinds of substances. The natural kind that consists not only of halogens, but of all the chemical elements, is more general still, and the elements in turn all have certain distinctive properties and some very general structural features that distinguish them from all other kinds of substances, and so on. As we ascend the natural kinds hierarchy, the behavioural and structural constraints on the more general kinds become progressively more relaxed. At the very highest level, there is a still more general kind, which we may call the "global kind". This is the category-wide kind, which includes every natural kind of object or substance that can exist in this world.

At each level, including the highest, there will be characteristic ways of behaving, due to the causal powers and propensities that distinguish the kinds of substances we are dealing with from all other kinds of substances. Moreover, at each level in the natural kinds hierarchy, including the highest, there will also be appropriately general kinds of structures. In the case of the global kind, the distinctive properties will be those that distinguish how the substances of this world, as opposed to those of any alien worlds (if such worlds should exist), are intrinsically disposed to behave, and the distinctive structures will include all those that are possible in worlds like ours. We should therefore expect to find that there are two natural hierarchies of laws: causal and structural. The most general causal laws will be those that apply indiscriminately to all substances in the world, whatever their specific natures. The conservation laws are good examples of laws of this kind, since the general form of every such law is: everything that can exist in this world is intrinsically conservative of X, where "X" names the conserved quantity. The most general structural principles will be those that must be satisfied by all possible structures of things in the kind of world in which we live. The principles of general relativity and of quantum mechanics are examples.

The proposed natural kinds structure of reality therefore has at least two very important consequences for Western philosophy, and ultimately for how we all think about the world. Not only does it undermine the modern subjectivist, relativist and anti-realist movements in philosophy by cutting the ground away from under them, but it also undermines what are currently the most widely accepted views about the status of the laws of nature, by arguing that these laws are not superimposed on the world, but grounded in the natures of the various kinds of things that exist. Even the most general laws of nature, it is argued, may have such a foundation, since they would appear to be distinguished only by the fact that they derive from the natures of the most general kinds of things.

The essentialist perspective on reality

The view that the laws of nature are immanent in the world derives from a recognition of its natural kinds structure, for the members of natural kinds are all bound to behave according to their natures. They cannot, unless they have somehow been de-natured, fail to act in these ways. Not even God, if there were such a being, could make them do otherwise. God could not make a hydrogen sample yield a chlorine spectrum, even if He were omnipotent. He might, conceivably, replace a hydrogen sample with a chlorine sample, and so make it appear to be yielding a chlorine spectrum. But, if this were possible at all, it would have to be a conjurer's trick, and not a genuine case of hydrogen producing such a spectrum.

To many, these remarks will seem highly counter-intuitive. We have become so used to the idea that God can perform miracles that this restriction on His power may well be seen as arbitrary. But from an essentialist viewpoint, this is not a restriction on God's power at all. God does not have the power to construct a triangle with four sides, not because His power is limited, but because it cannot be done. There is no such thing as a triangle with four sides. It is an impossible object. The same is true of hydrogen and its spectrum. God cannot make a sample of hydrogen that yields a chlorine spectrum, not because He lacks the power to do so, but because there is no such thing. There is no such thing as a sample of hydrogen that yields a chlorine spectrum. It is a metaphysical impossibility. If it is hydrogen, then it does not yield a chlorine spectrum, and if it does yield a chlorine spectrum, then it is not hydrogen, but chlorine. Or else it is just a trick, and not a genuine violation of the laws of chemistry.

The essentialist perspective on reality is therefore very different from the traditional one. From the point of view of a traditional passivist, anything can, in principle, be made to do anything at all by a being that is sufficiently powerful, for, according to passivism, the laws of nature are never metaphysical necessities. They are merely accidental regularities. Whatever the source of these regularities, whether it be God, the forces of nature or just brute fact, the laws themselves are contingent, and can, in principle, always be changed. Things that have always behaved in one way in the past, may, they argue, come to behave in very different ways in the future, not because they themselves have changed, but because the laws of nature have changed. From an essentialist perspective, however, the laws of nature are not contingent, but metaphysically necessary. Their necessity derives from the essential natures of the things on which they are said to operate. Essentialists say that the ways in which things are intrinsically disposed to act depend only on their causal powers, capacities and propensities. And, in so far as they may have any of these dispositional properties, essentially, they must, of metaphysical necessity, be disposed to act in precisely these ways, for their being so disposed is at least part of what makes them things of the kinds they are.

What is metaphysically necessary, essentialists say, is that things should be disposed to act in the manner required by their essential natures. This is not to say, however, that things cannot be prevented from so acting, or that the effect of their doing so cannot be swamped by other effects. The display of a causal power can be thwarted if intervention in the resulting causal process is possible – which indeed it often is. For example, if two barely sub-critical masses of U^{235} are on a collision course, then they will be disposed to produce an atomic explosion. But no explosion will occur if the masses are diverted at the last minute. Often the behaviour that is actually displayed on a given occasion may be the result of many different forces. Two massive objects are intrinsically disposed to attract each other, and must always do so according to the laws of gravity. However, if the masses are also electrically charged, firing rockets at each other and moving through a turbulent air-mass, then the actual behaviour of the masses will not be that predicted by the laws of gravity. It will be much more complicated than that. But these facts do not imply that the laws of nature are contingent. What is contingent is only whether the circumstances are apt for the causal powers of a thing to be clearly displayed.

CHAPTER 3

Properties and Relations

Introduction

To describe things in English, or in any other language, we must refer and classify. We may refer to things by naming, describing, or pointing to them, or by using a combination of these techniques. We may then describe them, or describe them further, by saying what they are like, or what they do, or something of the sort, and in doing so we inevitably classify them. The classifications that we make may have any of a number of different bases. Sometimes we classify things on the basis of some perceived similarity; ". . . is red" and ". . . is round" are two such classificatory expressions. Sometimes our classifications depend on some known similarity of function. The predicates ". . . is a table" and ". . . is a chair" are descriptive phrases used to classify things according to their functional roles. Sometimes things are classified according to what they do – when we say, for example, that someone is a professor or a butcher. Sometimes we classify things not according to what they are, or what they do, but, rather, according to what they are not, for example when we say of something that it is colourless, or non-English. There are many different techniques for securing reference, and there are probably hundreds of different bases for classifying things.

Moreover, classifications can be made of things in every different category of existence. We classify, and so characterize, objects, events, processes, properties, shapes, structures, substances, waves, thoughts, arguments and so on. Indeed, we must do so if we are ever to talk about any of these things, for that is how a descriptive language works; it works by saying what things are like, that is, by putting things that we think are similar in some way together under a common heading. Moreover, we recognize that there are similarities holding not only between individual things, but also in how these things can be related to each other. For example, the relationship ". . . is larger than . . ." is one that holds between Jupiter and Mars, Saturn and Venus, me and my granddaughter, and between millions of other such ordered pairs of objects. This is what is known as a two-part, or binary, relationship. Thousands of such relationships are recognized in all natural languages. There are also many three-part relationships, four-part relationships and so on. The possibilities are limitless. We are also able to recognize similar and dissimilar similarities, and consequently make a number of second-order classifications of things and relationships between things. So our language is classificatory through and through.

What is of most interest to essentialists are classifications based on supposed similarities of intrinsic nature. If two things are said to be square, for example, then these two things are thought to be intrinsically similar in a certain way. They not only affect us similarly, in that they look and feel as square things generally do, but they are presumably similar in themselves in some way, namely, in respect of shape. The same is not true of colour, however. If two things are said to be yellow, then certainly they are believed to affect us similarly, namely, by both appearing yellow to us under normal lighting conditions. But we are much less sure that there is any common basis for this similarity in the objects themselves, and quite sure that, if there is any common basis in the things themselves, it is nothing like the colour we perceive. There might, perhaps, be certain common atomic or molecular structures responsible for yellow colour perception. But probably even this is not true. There are transmitted, interference, diffracted and subjective colours, as well as ordinary reflected ones, and the processes that give rise to these colours are known to be very different from one another. So the evidence would appear to be that colour perception is a manner in which we are affected, rather than a representation in us of what exists in the objects we are perceiving.

Furthermore, the distinctions between the colours would appear to be mind-dependent, and so not anything that could exist in nature independently of us, or other creatures with minds. The visually discernible spectral colours each correspond to a (not very precisely specifiable) range of light frequencies, so that each can be produced by light of many different wavelengths. But the discernible spectral colours are only a small sample of all the colours we are able to distinguish visually, and no colour, whether spectral or otherwise, has a unique, or precisely defined, frequency and intensity profile. In fact, it is possible to match any observable colour in many different ways, choosing different combinations of light of different frequencies and intensities. It seems reasonable, therefore, to distinguish, as many philosophers have done before, between primary and secondary qualities. The primary qualities of things are those that are intrinsic to the objects that have them. The secondary qualities are the manners in which our senses are affected in the act of perceiving them.

In the modern era, this distinction was first made by Galileo,[6] although it was later developed by John Locke as one of the foundational doctrines of his empiricism. Galileo's statement of it is as clear as any. He wrote:

> whenever I conceive any material or corporeal substance, I immediately feel the need to think of it as bounded, and as having this or that shape; as being large or small in relation to other things, and in some specific place at any given time; as being in motion or at rest; as touching or not touching some other body; and as being one in number, or few, or many. From these conditions I cannot separate such a substance by any stretch of my imagination. But that it must be white or red, bitter or sweet, noisy or silent, and of sweet or foul odor, my mind does not feel compelled to bring in as necessary accompaniments. Without the senses as our guides, reason or imagination unaided would probably never arrive at qualities like these. Hence I think that tastes, odors, colors, and so on are no more than mere names so far as the object in which we place them is concerned, and that they reside only in the consciousness. Hence if the living creature were removed, all these qualities would be wiped away and annihilated. But since we have imposed upon them special names, distinct from those of the other and real qualities mentioned previously, we wish to believe that they really exist as actually different from those.   (G. Galilei 1623: 274–5)

Essentialists mostly accept the distinction between primary and secondary qualities, and the kind of account both Galileo and Locke gave of them. The primary qualities are properties of the objects themselves. The secondary qualities are manners in which we are

---

6. However, a similar distinction was made by the Greek atomist Democritus (b. 460BCE).

affected by things in the process of perceiving them.[7] But essentialists recognize another kind of property that is inherent in things, besides Locke's primary qualities – namely, a kind that includes causal powers, capacities and propensities. The original primary qualities were just those concerned with the structures of things, that is, with their shapes, sizes, states of aggregation and so on. In keeping with the mechanistic spirit of his age, Locke's list of primary qualities also included impenetrability, since (I suppose) he thought that no machine could possibly work if its parts were interpenetrable.[8] Causal powers, and other dispositional properties, were generally considered to be dependent on the laws of nature, and therefore not inherent just in the things themselves. The same things, Locke thought, could have different causal powers, depending on what the laws of nature are.

Properties and predicates

There is an important distinction between properties and predicates. Properties exist independently of language. They also exist independently of our knowledge, capacities, social practices and so on. That is, they are not mind-dependent entities, or social constructs, but things that exist independently of minds. Predicates, on the other hand, are purely linguistic items, and exist only as parts of a language. If there were no languages, there would still be plenty of properties, but there would be no predicates. It is true that predicates may sometimes be used to attribute properties to things, but that is not their only function, nor perhaps even their most important function.

---

7. Strictly speaking, Locke's secondary qualities included causal powers other than those that affect the senses directly, e.g. the power of one body to affect other bodies. He called them "causal powers mediately perceivable", and contrasted them with those that are "immediately perceivable" (Locke 1690: Bk. II, Ch. IX, §26). In this book, I shall reserve the name "secondary qualities" for those that are immediately perceivable. Causal powers of other kinds are fundamentally different from those that are immediately perceivable, and have a very important role in essentialist theory.

8. I am not sure why Locke chose to include impenetrability in his list of the primary qualities of matter. It has been suggested to me that it may be connected with the common seventeenth-century distinction between material and spiritual substances. Spiritual substances, the stuff of angels and minds, were thought not to be hindered by matter, but able to exist within it, or pass through it. Matter, on the other hand, was thought to be essentially impenetrable to other matter. Thus impenetrability was considered to be one of matter's most distinctive characteristics.

In general, predicates are linguistic devices for classifying things, on whatever basis; and, although classifications based on supposed intrinsic similarities are important in science, science is not everything. Properties, on the other hand, are genuine existents. They exist whether or not we know about them, or have any names for them. They are what Aristotle would have called "universals". They are instantiated in the things that have the properties, and they exist if just one instance of the property exists.

Properties are discovered by observing or studying nature, and sometimes these discoveries are made only with great difficulty. Scientists have indeed won Nobel prizes for discovering properties that were not previously known or suspected. There are properties that have no names – for example, because they have yet to be discovered – and there are predicates that truly apply to things, but do not name properties. Something can be red, for example, even though redness is not a property. It is not a property because it has no mind-independent existence. If the sentence "a is F" is true, then it is so because the object a satisfies the predicate "is F". That is, a belongs to the class of things picked out by this predicate. But this class of things is not necessarily a property class, that is, the class of things that have the property of being F, for there may be no such property.

Because of the preoccupation of English-speaking philosophers with language, this is an important point that needs to be vigorously stressed. Genuine properties are universals that are instantiated in the world. They are things that exist independently of language, and independently of human knowledge. Predicates, on the other hand, are just parts of sentences. They are embedded in languages, and would not exist if the languages in which they are embedded did not exist. The predicates of a language can have any of a wide range of functions, depending on what they apply to, and how they serve to classify these things. If a given predicate truly applies to some object, then it may be said to be *satisfied* by it. But there are all sorts of ways in which a predicate may truly apply to something, or, conversely, why an object may be satisfied by a given predicate. It depends on what role the predicate has in language.

Here are just some of the very many kinds of cases in which predicates are used for purposes other than to attribute properties to things.

- Some predicates are evaluative, like "... is good", "... is nasty" and "... is just", but there may be no properties of goodness, nastiness or justice that are attributed by their use. There are, no doubt, natural properties in virtue of which things are, or are judged to be, good, nasty or just. But these properties are not themselves goodness, nastiness or justice.

- Some predicates are used not to attribute natural properties to things, but rather to deny that things have certain properties. The predicates "is not spherical" and "is not at absolute zero", for example, do not denote properties, but signify that whatever properties their subjects may have, they are not these.
- Some monadic predicates, such as ". . . is under the apple tree" and ". . . is prehistoric" are really contracted relations, and do not denote properties in their own right.
- Some predicates, such as ". . . is legal" and ". . . is socially approved" apply to things in virtue of social conventions, attitudes or practices, and tell us more about society than about the things of which they are predicated.
- Existence is in a category of its own, and is often said not to be a property. However, ". . . exists" is grammatically a predicate, since it can sometimes be inserted after a proper name or a general name to make a true sentence. Whether existence is a property or not is, of course, arguable.
- Some predicates that can always be truly applied to things are obvious fabrications, and there is little temptation to say that they denote natural properties. The predicate ". . . is such that either p or not p" is a good example. Everything is such that either p or not p, and nothing is such that both p and not p. However, nothing is to be gained by postulating the existence of mad properties like these.

Of special interest are predicates with embedded conditionals, such as ". . . is disposed to do Y if X occurs". Opinion is divided about whether there are ever any natural properties (dispositional properties) denoted by such predicates. Many philosophers think there are no such properties. But essentialists argue otherwise. They think that there are indeed some genuine dispositional properties. The theory of dispositional properties will be taken up in the next section.

If there is no one–one correspondence between predicates that are true of things and properties, then the question of which predicates designate properties arises. As an essentialist, I answer: first decide what properties and structures you must postulate if you wish to give an adequate account of the phenomena, and then decide which expressions of the language refer to these properties or structures. Never try to argue from the fact that something is true of something that it denotes a property of it. This is really all there is to it. It follows that any two logically equivalent predications must refer to the same property or structure if either of them does. It also follows that no new properties or structures can ever be discovered simply by deduction from what is known to be true of things, for deduction is a linguistic operation, and it is always illegitimate to argue from language. From the fact that something is square, it can be deduced that it is either square or shiny. But it does not follow from this that there is a *property* of being either square or shiny. One would first have to have some independent reason for believing that there is such a property. From the fact that the object is square, it can be deduced that it is not round. But it does not follow from this that there is a property of being non-round. One would need some independent reason for believing this. If the object is not only square, but also made of copper, it follows logically that it is a copper square. But it does not follow that there is a property of being a copper square. There may or may not be such a property.

Most essentialists would probably agree with me about the illegitimacy of inferring the existence of disjunctive properties (such as that of being red or shiny), and of negative properties (such as that of being non-round), from the known existence of other properties (such as that of being square), but many would be prepared to allow that conjunctive properties may quite legitimately be inferred. However, I am unable to see any principled reason for accepting this inference, and I suspect that it is just a hangover from the standard practice of thinking that every predicate that is true of anything must name a property of that thing.

For similar reasons, I am not inclined to accept that there is a property of being a thing of a given kind, even though there are undoubtedly things of that kind. Is there, for example, a property of being a horse? Most philosophers, and perhaps even most essentialists, would answer "Yes", for certainly there are animals that are horses, and the predicate "is a horse" is true of this or that animal, although not of other animals. But it does not follow that there is a complex property, namely, that of being a horse, which all and only horses have, for one cannot legitimately infer the existence of a property (of being a horse) from the applicability of the predicate ("is a horse"). One does, it is true, have independent reasons for believing in the existence of horses. Their existence is not inferred just from the applicability of the predicate "is a horse". But there seems to be a crossing of conceptual boundaries here. My worry is not about the reality of horses, but about the conceptualization of horses as instances of complex properties. In general, properties are inherent in things, but their instances are not the things themselves. If there is a property of being a horse, then its instances are the things that are supposed to have this property, namely, the horses themselves. So, if there is such a property, then it is, to say the very least, a very peculiar property.

Inherent dispositional properties

On Locke's theory of qualities, the primary qualities of things are essentially passive and inherent in the objects themselves, and our mental representations of these qualities resemble the qualities themselves. The secondary qualities, on the other hand, were the qualities of sense experience, and our sense impressions were thought to be utterly unlike the arrangements and motions of the parts of things that he supposed were their intrinsic causes. The secondary qualities, he said, refer to the unknown causes of the kinds of sense impressions we have when we perceive things. The causal powers of things that are not immediately perceivable are different again. They describe the ways in which things are disposed to affect things other than the senses, and these qualities, Locke said, are known only indirectly through their effects on these things.

For Locke, causal powers whose effects are not immediately perceivable were of little interest, and he had almost nothing to say about them. They are barely mentioned in his *Essay*, and are not discussed in it. For essentialists, however, these, and other dispositional properties that are not immediately perceivable, include all of the sources of all power and order in the world, and, consequently, are absolutely central to their account of reality. Let us, therefore, reserve the term "causal powers" for the relevant species of these important, but much neglected, dispositional properties, and restrict the term "secondary qualities" to those whose effects are immediately perceivable. The causal powers, so understood, are objectively describable properties that are intrinsic to the objects that possess them. They are, therefore, at least as fundamental as the primary qualities were in Locke's scheme of things.

The class of properties that are neither primary qualities, in Locke's sense, nor immediately perceivable, includes several kinds other than causal powers. It also includes, for example, the intrinsic capacities of things to resist changes – that is, the properties that describe how things are disposed to resist causal influences of various kinds. Inertial mass, for example, is an intrinsic capacity, namely, the capacity of an object to resist acceleration by a given force. Moment of inertia, electrical resistance and Young's modulus are other capacities of this sort. But they are neither causal powers, nor Lockean primary qualities. The broader class also includes propensities of various kinds. The half-life of a particle is a measure of such a property. It measures the particle's intrinsic stability, by assigning a certain objective probability to the prospect of its decaying within a given period. An atom of a substance with a half-life of one year, for example, has an objective probability of precisely ½ of decaying within this period. Generally, the propensities of things describe the ways in which they are disposed to act, independently of causal influences. So they are not causal powers, as we have defined them; nor are they capacities, as this term is here understood. But like the others, propensities are dispositional properties, and causal powers, capacities and propensities all describe ways in which things are intrinsically disposed to act or interact.

With few, if any, exceptions, the fundamental properties of physical theory are all dispositional properties of the things that have them. They are either causal powers in the sense just defined, or else intrinsic capacities or propensities. Gravitational mass, for example, is a causal power: it is the power of an object to generate gravitational fields. Charge is a causal power: it is the power of a body to produce electromagnetic fields. The intrinsic angular momentum, or spin, of a particle is its power to contribute to the total angular momentum of a system. The materiality of a particle – its character as matter or antimatter – is an intrinsic property that distinguishes it categorically from its "mirror image" of opposite materiality, particles of opposite materiality being intrinsically disposed to annihilate each other.

These, and the other fundamental properties of particles, are known and distinguished from one another by what they do, and how things having these properties are intrinsically disposed to act or interact. None is passive in the sort of way that Locke's primary qualities were supposed to be. Mass acts in one way, charge in another, and spin in yet another way. The only one of Locke's primary qualities that is at all like any of these intrinsic dispositional properties is impenetrability, for impenetrability is the power of a body to resist penetration. In Locke's mechanistic universe, impenetrability does not come in degrees. If anything is a material substance then it is absolutely impenetrable. Penetration, as he understood it, is always a matter of pushing other material aside.

Essentialists differ importantly from most other philosophers in their attitudes to the dispositional properties of matter. For an essentialist, such properties may be fundamental, and not ontologically dependent on any other properties. For a passivist, such properties must always supervene on what they take to be the primary qualities of matter, and on the laws of nature. The idea that these properties might themselves be primary is firmly rejected.

Causal powers

According to essentialists, a causal power is a disposition to engage in a certain kind of process: a causal process. A causal process is one of a kind that relates two kinds of events. The first of these kinds of events, which we may call the "causal kind", includes all of the events that have the role of causes in these causal processes, and the second of these kinds, the "effectual kind", includes all of those events that have the role of effects in these processes. In every kind of causal process, there is a specific functional relationship between the causes and the effects, so that a given cause in the causal range produces a given effect (or probability distribution over a range of possible effects) in the effectual range. This is the causal relationship specific to this kind of process. It is usually quantitative, and, given suitable measuring conventions, able to be expressed mathematically.

According to David Hume, causal relations are relations between events. But they are relations that depend ultimately on relations between classes of similar events. We may define a cause, he said,

> to be *an object, followed by another, and where all the objects similar to the first are followed by objects similar to the second. Or in other words where, if the first object had not been, the second never had existed.*
>
> (Hume 1777: VII, II, 60, original emphasis)

By "objects" in this passage we may read "events", since the context makes it clear that this is what Hume intended. So, on this reading, Hume is saying that causal relations are primarily relations between classes of similar events. For an essentialist, however, the causal powers are primary. The regular patterns of behaviour that exist in the world, if they are not just matters of chance, are to be explained by reference to these powers. Therefore, causal relations cannot be reduced to mere instances of regularities, as Hume proposes. A causal relation could, for example, exist as a singular case, since such a relation will exist whenever any causal power is expressed, *even if that causal power happens never to be expressed on more than one occasion.*

Yet there is a sense in which Hume was almost right, because, if causal powers are dispositions to engage in causal processes of various kinds, then to define the causal powers of an object, we must specify the kinds of causal processes in which they could be involved. And, since any kind of causal process must involve a relationship between two kinds of events – between events of the causal kind, and events of the effectual kind – we can define a causal process if and only if we can define the relevant kinds of events, and then specify the causal relationship that holds between them. But we can do this objectively, that is, independently of how we may choose to classify things, if and only if all of the kinds of events and processes involved are natural kinds, that is, kinds of events or processes that exist as distinct kinds independently of human languages, perceptions, belief systems and so on. So the characteristic feature of all objective causal powers – powers that might well be intrinsic to the objects themselves – must be that their manifestations must always be events that belong to natural kinds. The secondary qualities are clearly not objective in this sense, because the display of any secondary quality, such as the power of an object to produce red visual sensations in us, is never an event that belongs to a natural kind. The objective causal powers of things are their dispositions to produce specific kinds of changes in the world, the distinctions between which, like the distinctions between the natural kinds, are categorical and absolute. They occur, and have the characteristics they have, independently of subjective human judgements. But the change that occurs in us when we see something red, although real enough, is not a display of any objective causal power. Rather, it is a combined, and perceptually filtered, effect of many different causal powers acting on us simultaneously.

Refraction, by contrast, is an objective causal process, the effect of which is not dependent on human perception or language. It is a process in which a beam of incident light (or other electromagnetic radiation) is bent as it passes through a surface from one medium into another. The angle of refraction for a beam of light of given frequency is a function of the refractive indices for that frequency of the two

media involved, and the angle of incidence of the beam. The phenomenon of refraction is, of course, well displayed by shining white light
through a prism to produce a rainbow-coloured spectrum. But this is
not essential to the process. Refraction occurs whenever electromagnetic radiation passes from one medium into another, whether or
not it is so clearly observable. It is a good example of a natural kind of
causal process, for it is one in which an event of a certain natural kind
(in this case, the falling of a ray of light on to the surface of a
transparent medium) produces a certain natural kind of effect (in this
case, the bending of the ray, in accordance with the law of refraction,
as it enters this medium). The causal powers responsible for this kind
of process are the refractivities of the two media involved.

Most causal processes are much more complex than this, and the
underlying objective causal processes may not always be visible. This
is because processes have a way of occurring one on top of another in
a kind of avalanche, obscuring each other's effects. The effect of one
causal process may even be to prevent another from occurring. (For
example, I may darken the room by pulling the curtains, thus prevent-
ing light from outside from coming in.) So causes may act either
positively or negatively. They may also act to obscure, reinforce,
inhibit, deflect or modify other effects, and so produce very complex
results that are not easily analysable. Nevertheless, there are some
cases where the causes are sufficiently cohesive, and the effects are
sufficiently clear, for a decent analysis of the objective causal processes involved to be possible. And, as you might expect, the clearest
examples of causal powers in action are often to be found in
chemistry. They are clear in this field of enquiry, because the
substances with which we have to deal are mostly highly purified, and
the circumstances in which the effects are produced are usually
contrived and clearly specifiable.

If essentialists are right about all this, then the consequences are
very great indeed, for the analysis clearly implies that the causal laws
supervene the causal powers of things – specifically, as the laws of
action of these powers. Humeans would have it the other way around.
From their point of view, the causal powers depend on the causal
laws. Moreover, if, as most essentialists believe, things may have
causal powers essentially, then the causal laws of action of these
properties must be the same in any world in which the things exist.
The laws are, therefore, necessary in the full-blooded metaphysical
sense of "necessity".

Intrinsic properties and structures

To discover the essential properties of any natural kind, we have to know where to look. One thing we know to start with is that the essential properties distinctive of any natural kind must be independent of the histories, locations and surroundings of its members. The essential properties of any member of a natural kind must therefore be among its intrinsic properties or structures. Most of us have a rough idea of what is meant by an intrinsic property or structure, and I have deliberately left this concept a bit vague until now. Roughly, it is a property that something has independently of any other thing. But it is hard to say much more precisely than this what an intrinsic property or structure is. Several philosophers have tried to do so, but their attempts have so far not succeeded, or not succeeded in explicating a concept that is of much relevance to the theory or practice of science. The problem is that the concept of intrinsicality that has mainly been sought is a *logical* one: the independence required for intrinsicality has been assumed to be *logical independence*. But what is needed for essentialism is a concept of *causal independence*.

For most philosophers, the current shape of a body is a property that it has intrinsically, because its current shape is logically independent of anything that exists externally to it. It is also logically independent of the shape it has had in the past, and of what its shape will be in future. However, the shape that an object has at a given time is not necessarily its natural shape. Normally, a solid body is distorted in various ways, by external forces, by internal forces arising from vibrations, or by inertial forces due to rotation or acceleration. In any such case, we say that the body is subject to stress and, consequently, that is in a state of strain. The natural shape of a body, by contrast, is the shape that it would have if it were not subject to stress. Engineers, and others who have to deal with solid materials, clearly must have some such concept in mind when they speak of a body being distorted, or in a state of strain, for nothing could be distorted, except with reference to some presumed undistorted state. For an essential-ist, this fact signals a much more interesting concept of intrinsicality than the logical one. Let us call it "causal intrinsicality".

The intrinsic shape of a stretched rubber band is not its actual shape, if by "intrinsic shape" we mean "natural shape", for the rubber band is distorted by the forces acting on it. It is elongated, and its sides are thinner than they would be if the rubber band were not being

51

stretched. But not everything that has such a shape is necessarily distorted. A steel band, for example, might be made as a model of a stretched rubber band, and have this shape naturally, independently of any accidental forces. Therefore, in the causal sense of "intrinsicality", the actual shape of a body may or may not be the same as its intrinsic shape. Its actual shape is best considered as being made up of two distinct parts: an underlying intrinsic shape, and a superimposed distortion.

In this same sense of intrinsicality, every body has a certain intrinsic mass. The actual mass of a body, for any given observer, is its mass relative to that observer. As with a body's shape, its actual mass may be analysed into two components: a rest mass, and a mass component due to the motion of the object relative to the observer. The rest mass of an object is its intrinsic mass, in the causal sense of "intrinsicality". It is the mass that the object would have if it were not in motion relative to us. The intrinsic spin of a particle is likewise one of its intrinsic properties, in the causally intrinsic sense, for this is the angular momentum component that is common to all particles of the same kind, whatever "motions" the particles may accidentally have. The total angular momentum of an orbital electron (within an atom), for example, is the vector sum of its orbital angular momentum and its intrinsic spin. Again, the half-life of a radioactive particle can vary with the frame of reference of the observer. A particle, such as a cosmic ray that is moving with very high velocity relative to us, may have a much longer half-life than one of the same natural kind with zero or near-zero velocity. Therefore, we may analyse the observed half-life of a particle as having two components: an intrinsic one, and a relativistic one.

Intrinsicality in the causal sense is therefore not a property of properties, as many of those who have tried to explicate a logical concept of intrinsicality have supposed. It has more to do with the role that the property has in physical theory. A causally intrinsic property is an underlying one that exists independently of us as observers. Most people these days are familiar with the idea of an underlying inflation rate, or an underlying employment rate. These concepts are introduced precisely in order to abstract the rates from any accidental market fluctuations that may have misleading implications. A causally intrinsic property is one that is underlying in this sense, although the abstraction from particular circumstances is made for somewhat different reasons. The observed shape or mass are real enough, but they are relative to the accidental circumstances under which the observations are made. The observed shape, for example, depends on the stress to which the object is subject, just as the observed mass depends on the velocity of the object whose mass is being measured. An essentialist who is seeking to describe the essential natures of things must seek a more objective standpoint, one that is independent of such accidental factors. And the only quantities that are independent of all such accidents are the causally intrinsic ones.

The concept of causal intrinsicality is not only required for an understanding of essentialism, but it is also one that has a fundamental role in scientific theory. From the viewpoint of essentialism, this is hardly surprising, since essentialism has been constructed as a metaphysic for scientific realism. Causal intrinsicality is important in science, because it reflects the structure of many scientific explanations. To explain the shape of the earth, for example, we must contrast its actual shape with the shape that it would have theoretically if it were not distorted by tidal forces, not rotating on its axis, not vibrating and so on. That is, we must contrast the earth's actual shape with what we conceive to be its intrinsic shape, and then explain the discrepancies. To explain the motion of a projectile, we must do something similar. We must analyse the motion to be explained as one that has both a natural part and a forced part. The natural part, which requires no force to sustain it, is assumed (or has been since Newton) to be a uniform straight-line motion. The forced part is then calculated as the difference between the actual motion and the supposed natural motion.

This model-theoretic pattern of explanation is absolutely standard in the physical sciences. It is not just a curiosity, or a pattern that is found only rarely, but one that occurs frequently in every field of science that purports to deal with natural kinds of objects or processes, and even in economics, where it does not. In all model-theoretic explanations, one attempts to abstract from the complex of forces acting on the system whose behaviour is to be analysed, in order to construct a theoretical model of how it would behave in the absence of these forces, thus allowing one to make use of various background theories. One then examines the actual system to see how it actually behaves, and how its actual behaviour differs from this theoretical ideal. The problem then is to explain the differences, for these differences are the effects that now require causal explanation. The gross behaviour of the whole system is not an effect that requires causal explanation because the gross behaviour of the whole system is not an effect at all. The effects to be explained causally are always just differences between what is actual and what is theoretical. The theoretical model we are using defines our concept of causal intrinsicality for the system we are dealing with, and this in turn defines the range of the effects that need to be causally explained.

Real essences

There are two classes of intrinsic properties and structures of things: those that they have necessarily, and those that they have only accidentally. Those that they have necessarily are the properties they must have, and cannot lose, without ceasing to be things of the kinds they are. Those that they have accidentally are those that they may or may not have, or may cease to have, without ceasing to be things of the kinds they are. The intrinsic properties that things have necessarily are their *essential properties*. Those that they may have, but need not have, are among their *accidental properties*. To illustrate, the essential properties of uranium are its atomic number, and the common electron shell structure for all uranium atoms, for these are the properties that every atom of uranium must have in virtue of being an atom of uranium, and which it could not lose without ceasing to be an atom of uranium. They are its essential properties. However, atoms of uranium also have some of their intrinsic properties only accidentally, for the atoms of this (or any other) element can always be in any of a number of states of excitation, depending on the energy levels that happen to be occupied by their orbital electrons. So it cannot be an essential property of a uranium atom that its state of excitation should be as it is.

But not all natural kinds are variable like this. There are some natural kinds whose members are necessarily intrinsically identical, that is, have none of their intrinsic properties accidentally. These are the "fixed natural kinds". The most elementary kinds of things that exist – for example, the fundamental particles – are all natural kinds of the fixed sort, for they all have fixed sets of intrinsic properties, all of which are essential to them. Why there should be such a distinction between kinds is not clear. The "variable natural kinds" – that is, those that, like a piece of iron, can exist in various states – are all somewhat more complex than the fixed ones. Perhaps the most fundamental natural kinds are fixed just because they have no fine structure to vary.

Whatever the reason, it is clear that most natural kinds are intrinsically variable, and, intuitively, that the degree of variability increases with the complexity of the kind. For the simplest natural kinds, the intrinsic properties are all essential properties. For natural kinds at the atomic, molecular and higher levels, the intrinsic properties and structures always include some states that are accidental. Nevertheless, the essential properties and structures are necessarily causally intrinsic. If the real essence of anything depended on its causally extrinsic or its relational properties, then a thing might cease to be a thing of the kind it is, not by undergoing any sort of intrinsic transformation, but because something else, or the circumstances, have changed. That atoms of uranium are to be found in the Jabiluka mine is true. But this cannot be what makes anything an atom of uranium. Indeed, if it were, then there would be no point in mining uranium at Jabiluka, because the mined material would have to cease to contain atoms of uranium the moment it was dug up.

This is not to say that extrinsic properties are never relevant to what things are called. On the contrary, the nominal essences of things – those properties or structures in virtue of which things are called what they are – often include such properties. The nominal essence of the aurora borealis, for example, includes its northern hemisphere location. In fact, the nominal essences of things are often not even properties, in the strict sense in which I am using this term, for things may well be, and often are, classified just on the basis of something that is merely true of them. We are free to classify things however we like, and on whatever basis we find convenient or useful. And, indeed, most of the classifications we make are not natural kinds classifications, or even classifications that are based on real properties. The nominal essence of a thing is therefore rarely the same as its real essence. The real essences of things are generally not the salient or superficial similarities between things that are likely to serve most of our purposes. It is mainly the purposes of science and of scientific understanding that are served by objective, or natural kinds, classifications.

There is a sense in which everything has a real essence, for there are always intrinsic properties or structures in virtue of which things have the manifest properties they have. These are roughly what Locke understood by the "real essences" of things. But these Lockean real essences may not be the same as the real essences of the natural kinds, for the question "In virtue of what intrinsic properties or structures is this thing a member of the natural kind it is?" is very different from Locke's question "In virtue of what intrinsic properties or structures does this particular thing have the manifest properties it has?" Locke's question (the second one) is focused on explaining the observable properties of particulars, not on discovering the essential properties of the kinds. When modern essentialists use the term "real essence", however, it is generally a kind essence to which they refer. Lockean real essences, which we might call "particular essences",[9] are of more interest to engineers than to physicists. If, for example, one is seeking the cause of a plane crash, then one might ask Locke's question. Assuming that the plane crash was due to an intrinsic weakness of some kind, what was the nature of this weakness, and how did it manifest itself? Physicists, on the other hand, usually have more general concerns. They might seek a general understanding of the phenomena of metal fatigue, but not of the specific causes of any particular structural failure. The physicists' real essences are not particular essences, but kind essences.

Quantitative properties

Most of the essential properties of things are quantitatively determinate properties. That is, they are the determinate values of the various quantities that are fundamental in nature. Unit mass m, for example, is the determinate value of the quantity *mass* that is possessed intrinsically by electrons. The mass M ($= 1836.12m$) is the determinate value of the quantity *mass* that is possessed intrinsically by protons. The charge e^- is the determinate value of the quantity *charge* that is possessed by electrons. The charge e^+ is the determinate value of the quantity that is possessed by both positrons and protons, and so on. Obviously, the basic quantities and their determinate values are fundamental in science. What can we say about them, and how do the quantitative hierarchies fit into the overall hierarchical structure of natural kinds?

Quantities, it is easily shown, are generic properties. For example, the quantitatively specific properties of having mass m, and of having mass M, are both species of the genus *mass*, for anything that has mass to any specific degree is clearly something that has mass. Moreover, nothing could have mass if it did not have it to some specific degree. The relationship between having mass, and having mass to this or that

---

9. There is another kind of essence to which particular essences are related, namely individual essences. This is the question: What is the source of any individual's identity? For example, one might ask: What makes this person the same as that person who lived here five years ago? But such questions will not occupy us here.

specific degree is thus, formally, a species relationship. Lions and domestic cats are both species of the genus *felis*. Consequently, any animal of either species is an animal of this genus. But also, if any animal is of the genus *felis*, then it is, necessarily, an animal that belongs to some species of this genus.

Many quantities are continuous: they have degrees that range over a continuum. Field strength, wavelength, temperature and many other quantities are like this. Other quantities are discrete: their specific values are discretely different from one another. Spin and charge, for example, are discrete quantities, and particles may differ from each other in either of these respects, but only by discrete amounts. The difference is unimportant from the perspective of essentialism. Continuous quantities are generic kinds too; it is just that their infimic[10] species form a continuum, rather than a discrete set. But if quantities are generic natural kinds that have specific quantitative properties as their infimic species, then what are their instances? It is easy enough to say what an instance of a natural kind of object is. It is an object of that kind – just as an instance of a natural kind of process is a process of that kind. But if a quantity is a generic kind, which stands to a set of specific quantitative properties as genus to species, then what are its members? They must be property instances. But what are property instances?

The property instances, or "tropes", as they are called, of any given property are the singular facts or states of affairs that must exist whenever, or wherever, this property is instantiated. And since properties are always instantiated in objects, their tropes must always be singular facts or states of affairs concerning these objects. It follows that a given property may have many different tropes, depending on how often, or in how many different places, it is instantiated. There are many different tropes of roundness, for example, because a great many things are round – snooker balls, dinner plates, coins and many other things – and tropes of roundness are located in all of them. Tropes of the property of being positively charged are likewise to be found in many different things: in protons, positrons and copper ions, for example. Indeed, there are as many tropes of this property as there are things that are positively charged.

If this analysis is accepted, then properties (and relations) may simply be regarded as natural kinds of tropes. The property of having unit mass, for example, will be the natural kind whose members are

---

10. An infimic species is a species that has no subspecies. It is ultimately specific.

all the tropes of unit mass, and the property of having positive charge will be the natural kind whose members are all the tropes of positive charge. Thus properties may be reduced to natural kinds of singular facts or states of affairs. So such singular facts or states of affairs are obviously very fundamental in ontology. Some philosophers have indeed been so impressed by this possibility, or by similar ones, that they have sought to reduce everything to singular facts or states of affairs.[11] However, it is beyond the scope of this book to investigate these systems.

---

11. Bertrand Russell and Ludwig Wittgenstein did so early in the century. Keith Campbell and David Armstrong are more recent advocates of ontologies of tropes or elementary states of affairs.

CHAPTER 4

Powers and Dispositions

Introduction

Essentialism presents a view of reality that is very different from that of any kind of passivism. Essentialists believe that:

(a) inanimate matter is not passive, but essentially active;
(b) the actions of things depend on their causal powers and other dispositional properties;
(c) dispositional properties are genuine properties, and intrinsic to the things that have them;
(d) the essential properties of things always include dispositional properties;
(e) elementary causal relations involve necessary connections between events, namely between the displays of dispositional properties and the circumstances that give rise to them;
(f) the laws of nature describe the ways that members of natural kinds are logically required (or are necessarily disposed) to act, given their essential natures; and
(g) the laws of nature are metaphysically necessary, because anything that belongs to a natural kind is logically required (or is necessarily disposed) to behave as its essential properties dictate.

These are all highly controversial theses that are anathema to most philosophers. Those I call "Humeans" would argue that:

(a) inanimate matter is essentially passive, never intrinsically active;

(b) things behave as they are required to by the laws of nature;
(c) the dispositional properties of things (including their causal powers) are not real properties, and are never intrinsic to the things that have them;
(d) the essential properties of things never include any dispositional ones;
(e) causal relations are always between logically independent events;
(f) the laws of nature are universal regularities imposed on things whose identities are independent of the laws; and
(g) the laws of nature are contingent, not necessary.

Evidently, many of the disagreements between essentialists and others hinge on their different conceptions of dispositional properties. Essentialists believe that there are genuine dispositional properties in the world, which are inherent in the things that have them. Passivists do not believe this, and are reductionist about dispositional properties. That is, they say that such "properties" are not real properties, and may be reduced to non-dispositional (i.e. categorical) properties and laws of nature. The root cause of this disagreement can be traced back to an even more fundamental one about the sources of power and activity in the world.

The dead world of mechanism

From the perspective of seventeenth- and eighteenth-century mechanism, the objective world is not intrinsically active. It is a world, according to Burtt, that is "hard, cold, colourless, silent, and dead; a world of quantity, a world of mathematically computable motions in mechanical regularity" (1932: 237). Descartes, Locke and Newton certainly believed something like this, as did most of their eighteenth-century followers. For Descartes, the essence of matter was just extension. It occupied space, and therefore had essentially only the attributes of things *vis-à-vis* their extension in space: shape, size and so on. For Boyle, Locke and Newton, the qualities inherent in bodies were just the primary qualities, namely number, figure, size, texture, motion and configuration of parts, impenetrability and, perhaps, body (or mass). If things with the same primary qualities were nevertheless different, then this difference must be due to differences in the primary qualities of, spatial relations between, or motions of, their elementary parts.

The qualities by which things are known to us are the qualities of experience: their colour, taste, warmth, odour, feel and so on. These qualities are known to us by the sensory ideas to which they give rise. Locke calls the powers that produce these sensory ideas the "secondary qualities". According to Locke (1690), these powers are not really inherent in the objects as they are in themselves. In themselves, the objects of experience have only the primary qualities. Nor can the sensory ideas be supposed to resemble, in any way, the powers of the objects to induce them in us, for these powers must be supposed to be grounded solely in the primary qualities of the insensible parts of these objects, which are of an altogether different character from any of the ideas they furnish.

Locke distinguished two kinds of powers: active and passive. The active ones are the powers of things to *make* changes; the passive ones are the abilities of things to *receive* changes (Locke 1690: 234). God, he supposed, had only active powers. Inanimate things, he speculated, may have only passive ones. If this is right, then created spirits, such as ourselves, would be the only things to have both active and passive powers. When we exercise our free will in some voluntary action, we certainly display an active power, according to Locke. Hence, there is no doubt, he thought, that human beings, *qua* created spirits, have active powers. But also, when we perceive anything we display our capacity to be affected by it. So it is evident that, *qua* created spirits, we also have passive powers.

The question of importance in the present context is whether active powers exist in inanimate nature. What Locke believed about this is a question of scholarship that need not concern us. But certainly a great many seventeenth- and eighteenth-century mechanists did believe in the complete passivity of inanimate nature. If one object seems to affect another, for example crash into it and so cause it to move, then what is involved is not so much an *action* on the part of the first body as a *passion*. As Locke explained:

A Body at rest affords us no *Idea* of any *active Power* to move; and when it is set in motion it self, that Motion is rather a Passion, than an Action in it. For when the Ball obeys the stroke of a Billiard-stick, it is not any action of the Ball, but a bare passion: Also when by impulse it sets another Ball in motion, that lay in its way, it only communicates the motion it had received from another, and loses in it self so much, as the other received; which gives us but a very obscure *Idea* of *active Power*, which reaches

61

not the Production of the Action, but the Continuation of the
Passion.   (1690: 235, original emphasis)

Perhaps the mathematician Leonhard Euler adequately represents
mid-eighteenth-century views on causal powers. In his *Letters to a
German Princess* (1795), written in the early 1760s, he addressed at
length the question of what kinds of powers exist in the world, and
what their sources are (vol. 1, 295–340). He argued, as Locke had
speculated, that the powers existing in inanimate nature are all
essentially passive. Indeed, he thought that the powers necessary for
the maintenance of the changing universe would turn out to be just
the passive ones of inertia and impenetrability. There are no active
powers, he argued, other than those of God and living beings.
Consequently, if the mechanist's world-view is correct, the myriad
changes that we see occurring around us must all be consequential
upon the inertial motions of things, and their mutual impenetrabil-
ities. The so-called forces of nature, for example gravitational
attraction, may describe the ways in which things are *disposed* to
behave *vis-à-vis* each other. There is no doubt that things are disposed
to accelerate towards each other as the laws of gravity and motion
require. But the source of that disposition, he argued, is not an
attractive force emanating from the bodies, or just a natural tendency
of bodies to move according to the dictates of some pre-established
harmony, as Leibniz believed, but an impulsion of one thing towards
another produced by some kind of tension in the ether. When the
nature of this process is fully understood, Euler supposed, the
planetary motions, and gravitational accelerations generally, would
all be seen to be the passive consequences of inertia and mutual
impenetrability.

Plausible as some of the mechanists' arguments for this conclusion
may have been, it is to be argued here that this is a radically incorrect
view of the nature of reality. The real world is essentially active and
interactive. It is not passive, as the old mechanists believed, and the
neo-mechanists of today also believe. It is dynamic. And its dynamism
stems from the existence of genuine causal powers in things, both
active and passive. Locke, Euler and the other mechanists of the
period all believed in the essential passivity of nature. But they were
wrong, or so I shall argue. The inanimate world is not passive, as they
believed. Material things do have causal powers, which, in appropriate circumstances, they will exercise; and these causal powers are real
occurrent properties of the things in question.

Scientists today certainly talk about inanimate things as though they believed they had such powers. Negatively charged particles have the power to attract positively charged ones. Electrostatic fields have the power to modify spectral lines. Sulphuric acid has the power to dissolve copper. The question we have to consider in this chapter is what is the source of these powers? The old mechanist view was that *things* do not *themselves* have causal powers. The powers lie outside them. They are contained in the forces that act externally on things to change their states of motion or aggregation.

Forces as external to objects

The mechanists of the seventeenth and eighteenth centuries all believed in the mechanical nature of change. That is, they thought that all changes must ultimately be just changes of position, or changes in the states of motion of things. If a thing changes shape, for example, then its parts must change their positions in relation to one another. If it explodes, then its parts have been caused somehow to become rapidly separated, and consequently move rapidly away from each other. If a thing changes colour, it was supposed, then this too must ultimately be due to some change in the arrangement of its parts. And similarly for any other change that might occur. The elementary parts of things were all thought to be rigid and unchanging, and to be distinguished from each other only by their shapes, sizes and the like. But these ultimate constituents of matter, they thought, could not change. So all changes, it was supposed, must consist of only changes in the arrangements or motions of these most elementary things.

Forces were postulated as elementary causal links between things for the purpose of explaining the changes that take place. The forces were not, however, thought to change the elementary things themselves, but only how they move or are arranged, for the identities of the elementary things were considered to be independent of the forces that operate on them, and the forces were always thought to be external to objects on which they directly impinge. So the picture was one of intrinsically rigid bodies being pushed or pulled around by the forces of nature acting on them. Even the forces of cohesion, which hold the parts of bodies together, were considered to be really external. They might be internal to the bodies themselves, but they are external to the parts of the bodies on which they directly operate.

Given this conception of reality, it is clear that the forces are the sources of all power and order in the world, and that these are supposed to exist externally to the things they affect, just as in the divine command theory. Thus passivism is a natural consequence of mechanism. Change the forces, or change the laws of nature so that new forces may come to act between things, and the same elementary things will be disposed to behave in different ways. The dispositions of things must therefore all depend ultimately on the underlying structures of the elementary things of which they are composed, and on the laws of nature that determine what forces there are, and how they operate on these most elementary things. This, with perhaps a few concessions to modernity, is the doctrine known as "categorical realism".

Mechanists assumed the identities of things to be independent of any forces they may be said to generate. Indeed, the most widely accepted view was that inanimate things could not generate any forces at all, for that would imply that they had active powers, which, by their inanimate nature, they could not possess. Yet things do at least appear to have some active powers, and various kinds of forces (e.g. gravitational, electric and magnetic) were recognized. Consequently, the natural philosophers of the period all used the language of active causal powers quite freely in their descriptions of inanimate nature, even if they believed that these powers were ultimately not active, but passive. If pressed, they would say that the powers were not really inherent in the objects that seemed to possess them, but were dependent on their ultimate constitutions, and on the laws of nature, which were universally supposed to be external to them.

For these reasons, causal powers, and forces generally, were regarded as occult. Hume went so far as to deny that there existed in nature anything other than the regular patterns of behaviour that explanations in terms of forces were intended to explain; and when we speak of causes, he said, it is really only to such regularities that we can be referring.

Consequently, propositions attributing causal powers to things have long been regarded with suspicion. And this suspicion applies not only to active causal powers (those which are not obviously dependent on the actions of God or man), but also to the passive ones, for the two go together. For every passive causal power – that is, power to *receive* change – which is ever exercised by anything, there must be an active causal power – power to *make* changes – to which it is responding. Consequently, if one kind of power is suspect, then so is the other. If the power to produce a change is no more than an invariable disposition of something to behave in a certain way in certain circumstances, then the power to receive change can be no more than an invariable disposition of something to respond in a certain way in these circumstances. But such invariable dispositions are not thought to be real properties of the things in question. The real properties are just the underlying structures to which the laws of nature may be supposed to apply.

Dispositions and causal processes

Information about the dispositions of things tells us about what they are likely to do, or how they are likely to react, in various kinds of circumstances. It is, therefore, information about how things affect, or are affected by, things. Most dispositions that are discussed in the literature are concerned with causal relations between two or more things, although there are some dispositions, such as that of a radio-active substance to decay, that are not. Water-solubility, toxicity and brittleness are often cited as examples in the literature. Each of these dispositions is concerned with a kind of causal process, and may be identified with a kind of causal power or capacity or liability, depending on point of view, and on what role in the process it is seen as having. Thus, if something is water-soluble, then it has the capacity to dissolve in water. If it is toxic, then ingesting it may well cause one to become ill or die. If it is brittle, then, if it is given a sharp shock, or otherwise handled roughly, it is liable to shatter or snap. Each of these is a disposition of something to act or react in a certain kind of way. It is also a disposition that can be expected to be displayed in certain kinds of circumstances. The circumstances in which a disposition would be displayed are called the "triggering" circumstances.

The distinctions between causal powers, capacities, propensities, liabilities and so on, which appear to name different species of dispositions, are difficult to make, and of doubtful philosophical significance. What we think of as a causal power occupies the role of driving force in a causal relation. But many dispositions that we think of as causal powers might equally well be regarded as capacities (a term that is more or less neutral between activity and passivity), or even as liabilities. If causal powers are dispositions to affect other things in certain kinds of ways, then liabilities are dispositions to be affected by other things. If something is brittle, for example, then it is liable to break. But not all causal processes are as straightforwardly directed as some of these standard examples suggest, and in many cases it is much more natural to think of the causal processes involved as causal interactions, where each participant may be thought to be both active and reactive. Water-solubility, for example, is as much a power as a liability. It can be thought of as the power of the substance to dissolve into the water. Or, equivalently, it can be regarded as a liability to be dissolved by it. Clearly, both solute and solvent have some kind of causal power or capacity in relation to the other, even though there is no clear direction of causal influence.

This much is all more or less common ground, but philosophers disagree strongly about how the dispositions of things are to be explained, for they have different theories of causation; and how one thinks about dispositions depends largely on how one thinks about causal relations. For Newtonians, and other mechanists, a causal relation is one that is mediated in a certain way by the action of forces between two states of affairs. Therefore, given this conception of causation, the dispositions of things must depend on what forces exist, and how they act. If the laws of nature were different, and different forces consequently existed, then the dispositions of things would also be different. For Hume, and for all latter-day Humeans, an instance of causation is just an instance of a universal regularity of some kind. Therefore, if the laws of nature were different, and the regularities that existed were consequently different, the dispositions of things would no longer be the same. For essentialists, however, the dispositions of things depend on the intrinsic causal powers or capacities of their most basic constituents, and on how these constituents are arranged. Consequently, the dispositions of things cannot be varied, except by changing their constitutions in some way, so that they cease to be things of the kinds they are.

The kinds of dispositions that are named in English, and in other languages, often refer to clusters of causal processes that are grouped together by us as having similar effects. For example, many different kinds of things may be said to be fragile, and this dispositional term may be applied to almost anything that is easily destroyed or broken. Thus we have fragile vases, parchments, spiders' webs, eco-systems and personalities. But no one imagines that things of these diverse kinds have a genuine common property of fragility. There are, in fact, many different properties or structures that make for fragility, and they are mostly very different from one another. This being the case, it is implausible to suppose that the predicate ". . . is fragile" names a real property. In general, one must always be careful not to be too influenced by the occurrence of a common name. A common name may signify a common reason for interest, or a similar evaluation of something. But it is not, in itself, good evidence for the existence of a common property.

But not all dispositions of the kinds that we can name in our language are like fragility. Many of them are due to genuinely similar properties. Acids, for example, have something in common in virtue of which they are acidic. Alkalis have something in common in virtue of which they are alkaline. Electrons have something in common in virtue of which they have the same power to generate electromagnetic fields. In each case, the things classified together as being of the same kind are so classified because they have the same or similar causal powers. All electrons have the same capacity to generate electromagnetic fields. All acids have a similar capacity to supply protons in chemical reactions.

Essentialists argue that these causal powers are genuine properties, or kinds of properties. The charge on an electron, they say, is a genuine property of the electron, and not a property that it happens to have just because of its non-dispositional properties, and what the laws of nature happen to be. The acidity of a solution, they say, is a genuine property of that solution, and acidity in general is a kind of property that is shared by many different substances. Moreover, acidity is not a property that could be changed just by changing the laws of nature. For the same substances, they would argue, would be acidic in any world in which they might exist. Essentialists call such properties as charge and acidity "dispositional properties", because they are properties whose identities depend on what they dispose their bearers to do.

The dispositional properties that exist in nature are all associated with natural kinds of causal processes. To say that an object has a specific dispositional property is to say that it is intrinsically disposed to participate in natural causal processes of the kind that are associated with that specific property. To say that is has some generic dispositional property is just to say that it is intrinsically disposed to participate in causal processes of the generic kind associated with that generic property. It is plausible, therefore, to think of a dispositional property as a relationship (of potential instantiation) between an object (its bearer) and a natural kind of process (the kind of causal process involved in its display). In classical Greek metaphysics, properties were thought of as universals that are instantiated in the things that have these properties. In modern essentialist metaphysics, dispositional properties are dynamic universals (i.e. natural kinds of processes) that are potentially instantiated in the things that have these dispositional properties. But more on this later.

Categorical and dispositional properties

There is an important distinction in the literature between categorical properties and dispositions. Categorical properties are thought of as properties that things may have independently of how they may be disposed to behave: they are considered to be essentially non-dispositional. Dispositions, on the other hand, are supposed to be essentially dependent on how things are disposed to behave in various possible circumstances. So there is, apparently, a sharp distinction between the two kinds of properties. However, it is not entirely clear which properties are dispositional and which are not, for every property must be capable of manifesting itself to us in some way or other; otherwise we could never know about it. It is easier to say what categorical properties are not, than what they are, for whatever they are, they are not causal powers or capacities of any kind, because causal powers and capacities are all essentially dispositional. That is, their identities depend on the kinds of circumstances in which they would be displayed, and how they would be displayed in each of these kinds of circumstances. The categorical properties, on the other hand, are thought to be properties of a different kind, which are intrinsically different from each other, and whose identities depend on *what* they are, rather than on how they dispose their bearers to behave. The Lockean primary qualities of shape and size, for example, and also the various structural properties of things, are often cited as examples of categorical properties.

The so-called categorical properties all have this at least in common: they are readily imaginable. Things having these properties can always be pictured or drawn, and if different colours are used for different substances, then complex structures of atoms or molecules of different kinds can also be represented in our imaginations. So it is easy to think that such structures might exist independently of any patterns of behaviour by which they might be known. Dispositions, on the other hand, cannot be pictured, except in action. There are not enough visually distinguishable colours in the rainbow for us to use a distinctive colour for each distinct dispositional property.

Categorical properties are also, in a sense, multi-dimensional. All of the exemplary categorical properties may be pictured as structures in two or more dimensions. Other properties, such as refractivity, elasticity, magnetic permeability, heat capacity, torsion modulus and the like, which cannot be so pictured, are generally considered to be dispositional. Because these properties are one-dimensional, the differences between them do not depend on any *imaginable* differences between states of affairs. Pictures of things differing from each other in respect of these various properties might all *look* exactly the same (although the view through two things of different refractive index might look a bit different). We might be able to distinguish between them in our imaginations by using some colouring or shading conventions. But this would clearly be highly artificial. One may be inclined to suppose that the same must be true of all intensive magnitudes. But temperature differences may clearly be regarded as categorical differences, since the different states of agitation of the molecular structures are easy enough to picture.

The distinction between dispositional and categorical may thus appear to be very superficial, for what is able to be pictured or imaginable is hardly what counts in ontology, and if this were the only basis for the distinction, then there would not be much of a case for it. However, there are independent reasons for thinking that structural properties are different from non-structural ones. First, there are "block structures". Block structural properties are properties that depend on relations between things that have identities independently of these relations. They are properties that exist if and only if the constituent things exist and are related in the appropriate ways. A molecular structure, for example, is a block structure. It exists if and only if the constituent atoms of this structure exist and are related in the appropriate manner for this molecular structure. Moreover, these atoms themselves have block structures that exist if and only if there are subatomic particles that are related in the manner appropriate for atoms of these kinds. Now these block structural properties are clearly not just dispositional. It may be true that an atomic or a molecular structure of a given kind exists if and only if there is some atom or molecule that is disposed to behave in a certain way in appropriately specified conditions. But this is not what makes it an atom or molecule of this kind. Its essence is structural, not dispositional. It is, of course, only from the behaviour of an atom or molecule that we can infer its structure. But the structure exists independently of its disposition to behave in this way.

Secondly, there are intrinsic structures. These are the structures of fields, of the quantum vacuum, of space-time and so on. These structures are not made up of parts that are capable of independent existence, as the block structures are. Nevertheless, there is a clear sense in which they are structures, for they are all spatiotemporal distributions of (statistical) causal powers (in the broad sense in which this term is here being used). To take a classic example, the electro-magnetic field, which is described by Maxwell's equations, is an intrinsic structure of electric and magnetic potentials. A knowledge of these equations, and of the boundary conditions of a given field, enables us (in principle) to determine the magnitudes, directions and spatiotemporal distributions of electrical and magnetic forces that would operate in this field. But the parts of this structure are incapable of existing independently of it. And the same is true generally of all intrinsic structures. They are dispositional property structures.

It is reasonable to accept, therefore, that there is an important distinction between categorical and dispositional properties, although this view is not generally shared by essentialists. The categorical properties are structural, I want to say, in one or other of these two senses, and their essences are not dispositional. The dispositional properties are not structural, however, and their essences lie in the dispositions they sustain.

However, if this is the correct basis for the distinction between categorical and dispositional properties, then the categorical properties in nature must all be ontologically dependent on the dispositional ones, and on the spatial, temporal or other relations that may exist between things whose essential properties are purely dispositional. In other words, the basis for the distinction between categorical and dispositional properties implies that dispositional properties and structural relations are ultimately fundamental.

Categorical realism

Probably the most widely accepted theory of dispositions is "categorical realism", for this is the only theory of dispositions that passivists can readily accept. Categorical realists believe that the fundamental properties of nature are all categorical, and that the dispositional properties of things all supervene on their categorical ones. The dispositional properties, they argue, all depend on the laws of nature, which tell us how things in nature are naturally disposed to behave. The things themselves, they say, must be entirely neutral about this. They cannot, by their own natures, be required to act in one way rather than another, because it is the prerogative of the laws of nature to determine how they must behave. On the other hand, the things in nature cannot be entirely lacking in properties, unless one can believe in "bare particulars". So the intrinsic properties of things in nature must all be categorical. They cannot have any dispositional properties essentially.

It is plausible to suppose that categorical realists take this position on dispositional properties mainly because an ontology of primitive dispositional properties must be incompatible with passivism, for to believe that the most fundamental properties in nature are dispositional rather than categorical is to believe that things in nature are essentially active and reactive. It is to accept an ontology of causal powers, capacities and propensities, rather than one that is passive, as Locke's and Hume's ontologies were.

But the reasons for belief in categorical realism are really much more complicated than this. It is not just a one-step inference from passivism, for categorical realism is just one aspect of a very large complex of more or less consistent views about the nature of reality – one that has been thoroughly investigated by philosophers over the centuries, and holds a special place in Western philosophy. It is the established metaphysic of our culture. It embraces the whole system of beliefs described at the beginning of this chapter, and many others besides. It is the metaphysical position that I call "Humeanism", not because Hume invented it, but because he probably did more than anyone else to articulate it.

One aspect of Humeanism that is important in this context is its strong commitment to the contingency of the laws of nature: to the thesis that these laws could have been other than they are. This is now generally known as the "contingency thesis". The contingency thesis has a very long history, for it was already implicit in the divine command theory that was widely accepted in the Middle Ages. If God makes the laws of nature, as theists of those times generally believed, then God can unmake them, or change them. They are, after all, supposed to be at His command. Indeed, if God could not change the laws of nature at will, then He could not perform miracles either, and to say that would be heresy.

The contingency thesis is not, however, basically a theological doctrine, and it easily survived both the scientific revolution of the

71

seventeenth century and the Enlightenment of the eighteenth. With the exception of Leibniz, every Western philosopher of note in this era believed in the contingency of laws of nature, and most philosophers today still do. Philosophers then and since have disagreed about the nature of causation, and hence about causal laws. Some, whom I call Newtonians, believed that all causes are mediated by forces. But the causal laws were still held to be contingent, for what forces there are was said to be a contingent matter. Thus, the contingency thesis about the causal laws just became a contingency thesis about the forces acting. God might not be able to change the way in which a given force acts, but He could surely bring other forces into play, or remove any of the ones that were already operative. Other philosophers, most notably Hume and his followers, thought that forces were unintelligible entities that contributed nothing to our understanding of causation. There are no forces, he argued, nor any other necessary connections in nature, but only some regular sequences of events. Properly understood, he said, causal laws are nothing more than universal regularities of some kind, and causes are just instances of such regularities. These Humean theses are known as the "regularity theories" of laws and of causation.

Categorical realists mostly operate in this tradition, although new and much more interesting theories of laws and causation have recently been developed, and defended along with categorical realism. All of them, however, accept the contingency thesis. Categorical realists are thus agreed that dispositions depend on the causal laws of nature, and that these laws are all contingent. Therefore, they argue, it is possible for the causal laws, and hence the dispositions of things, to be different from what they are. In some worlds (such as ours), for example, ethylene freezes at a lower temperature than water. But, say the categorical realists, there must be other possible worlds in which ethylene freezes at a higher temperature. Therefore, they would argue, the disposition of ethylene to freeze at a lower temperature than water must be world-dependent. It must depend on what the laws of nature happen to be in the world in question. And the same, they would say, must be true of all dispositions. If something has a certain disposition in this world, then, necessarily, there is another possible world in which it (or its identical counterpart) does not have this disposition. What is brittle here might well not be brittle there. Hence, the identity of a thing cannot depend on its dispositions; it can only depend on its categorical properties. The dispositions of things cannot be of their essence, because all dispositions depend on what

72

the laws of nature are, and these laws are all contingent and extrinsic to the things on which they operate.

If the dispositions of things may thus vary from world to world, depending on what the laws of nature are for the different worlds, then, we must ask, what grounds them in the specific things? What makes one thing have a given disposition while another lacks it? Presumably, each disposition has some kind of basis in the things that have it. Presumably, one disposition could depend on others. But, ultimately, the categorical realists say, the manifest dispositions of things must be grounded in the categorical properties of the things that have them. Otherwise, their existence would be inexplicable. A metaphysical wedge is thus driven between the dispositions of things and the real properties of the things that have them. Given that the laws of nature are contingent, the relationship between a given disposition and the categorical properties that are supposed to ground it must also be contingent, and hence the grounding properties and the disposition must be ontologically distinct from each other. If this is right, then we are free to associate dispositions with categorical bases according to how the laws are in each possible world, thus ensuring that objects that are disposed to behave in a particular way in a given world are said to have the dispositions that correctly describe their behaviour.

The main arguments in favour of the categorical realist's claim that dispositions need categorical bases are that they are needed to explain the continuing existence of, and also the differences between, dispositions that are not currently (and perhaps never have been, and never will be) manifested. These are the "continuing existence" and the "difference" arguments.

The continuing existence argument is this: (1) Dispositions continue to exist unmanifested. (2) The fact that dispositions continue to exist unmanifested needs explanation. (3) The continued existence of a disposition would be explained if it had a purely categorical basis, for the continued existence of such a basis needs no explanation. (4) The continued existence of a disposition cannot be explained in any other way. Therefore, (5) dispositions must ultimately have categorical bases. There is, however, no good reason to believe that dispositional properties cannot be fundamental, and therefore capable of existing and continuing to exist unmanifested. The fact that dispositional properties cannot be pictured, as categorical properties can be, is no good reason to think that they cannot exist fundamentally. On the contrary, there is every good reason to believe that the most fundamental properties in nature are causal powers, capacities and propensities, and the fact that we cannot picture them is irrelevant.

The difference argument is more interesting. It is the argument to the effect that if two things differ in respect of any of their dispositions, they must also differ in respect of at least one of their non-dispositional properties. Otherwise, the difference would be inexplicable. The argument is interesting because its premise seems quite plausible. If two things differ in respect of any of their dispositions, then surely there must be a difference elsewhere that would explain this difference. But why must it be supposed that the only possible explaining difference is one of categorical properties? Why could the explaining difference not be one of dispositional properties? Unless one is already of a mind to think that the only real properties are the categorical ones, the difference argument has no force. One could accept that there must be some other difference, but deny that this difference must be categorical.

It is true, of course, that dispositions need to be based in reality. They must always be grounded in real properties. The only question concerns the nature of these real properties. Categorical realists say that the only real properties are the categorical ones. Essentialists take the view that the real properties – for example, causal powers, capacities or propensities – may be dispositional. That is, they are dispositional realists. The question is, then, whether the main arguments for categorical realism are persuasive. I think not, for both arguments rely on the assumption that real properties are able to be visualized or represented in our imaginations. But this is an assumption for which there appears to be no justification. No unidimensional properties, and surely there are many, are going to be able to be visualized in the sort of ways that shape, size or structures are. There are just differences of degree for such properties, and the only way in which they could possibly be pictured would be by adopting some convention (e.g. of shading or colouring) to do so. But why should that count against them? On the contrary, it is much more plausible to suppose that the most basic properties are the underlying quantitative ones that dispositional realists believe in. And these, by their nature, cannot be represented directly in our imaginations.

If the arguments in favour of categorical realism are weak, those in favour of dispositional realism are fairly strong. First, there is the argument from science. The most fundamental things that we know about all have causal powers or other dispositional properties, and, as far as we know, they only have such properties. Of course, it could be that they have structures that we do not know about, which are somehow responsible for their dispositional properties, but there is nothing that suggests that this might be so, and there is even less reason to believe that the causal powers or propensities of the most basic things in nature are ontologically dependent on these supposed underlying structures. On the contrary, block structures are not ontologically primary, since they are dependent on the existence of their parts, and intrinsic structures are spatiotemporal structures of dispositional properties.

Secondly, there is the argument from the nature of the laws of nature. The laws do not merely describe the behavioural regularities of things that are characterized by their categorical properties alone. On the contrary, the laws of nature appear more often to be concerned with properties that are not structural. There are no known laws of nature that are concerned with the shapes or sizes of things, and those that are concerned with block structures are dependent on the dispositional properties of their component parts. Most laws of nature, it seems, are concerned with quantitative dispositional properties such as mass, charge, magnetic field strength, moment of inertia, specific heat, energy density, potential energy, half-lives or how the various forces of nature would operate to affect things. Or, at a more fundamental level, the laws of nature are concerned with what causal interactions are possible, with what probabilities they would occur, and what quantities would be conserved in these interactions. Dispositional concepts thus occur essentially in the laws of nature, as far as we know them. Therefore, laws of nature of the sort that categorical realists would need to effect their ontological reductions of dispositional properties simply do not exist. There are no known regularities of behaviour that are specific to things of a given shape or size, for example, or to the members of the extensions of any other categorical property. In chemistry, there are laws that plausibly just describe how substances of various kinds interact, but these laws do not express mere regularities. On the contrary, they make use of precisely the kinds of dispositional concepts that categorical realists seek to reduce. That salt dissolves in water, for example, or that hydrogen is exploded by a spark in oxygen to form water, are laws that, perhaps more plausibly than most, are just statements of regularities. But the laws that underlie these regularities are dispositional, for what has to be explained in these cases is the *solubility* of salt in water, or the *potential* for hydrogen and oxygen to combine explosively to form water.

Thirdly, there is the ontological regress argument. Whenever a causal power is seen to depend on other properties, these other properties must always include causal powers, for the causal powers of things cannot be explained, except with reference to things that themselves have causal powers. Structures are not causal powers, so no causal powers can be explained just by reference to structures. For example, the existence of planes in a crystal structure does not by itself explain the crystal's brittleness, unless these planes are cleavage planes: regions of structural weakness along which the crystal is disposed to crack. But the property of having such a structural weakness is a dispositional property that depends on the fact that the bonding forces between the crystal faces at this plane are less than those that act elsewhere to hold the crystal together. Therefore, the dispositional property of brittleness in a crystal depends not only on the crystal's structure, but also on the cohesive powers of its atomic or molecular constituents.

However, cohesive powers are causal powers. They are the forces that bind things together. For a crystalline structure, these forces are presumably electromagnetic, and therefore depend on the dispositions of charged particles to interact with each other in the sorts of circumstances that exist inside a crystal. To explain the distribution of the cohesive forces existing in such circumstances, the structure of the crystal must be described in some detail. But this description will not by itself do anything to explain the cohesion of the parts of the crystal. To do this, it is also necessary to say what energy states are occupied by the structure's various constituents, and to specify their dispositions to resist being prised out of their respective positions. So cohesive powers have to be explained in terms of other causal powers. And there never seems to be any point at which causal powers can just drop out of the account.

An analysis of dispositions

What, then, are dispositions and dispositional properties? I have so far used these terms fairly loosely and intuitively. Let us now try to be a little more precise. When I speak of the dispositions of things, I am talking about how these things will, or be likely to, behave in various kinds of circumstances. I am not diagnosing the causes of this behaviour. But when I speak of the dispositional properties of things, I am talking about what I believe to be genuine properties, rather than just behavioural tendencies: properties that I take to be of the nature of causal powers or capacities of some sort.

Dispositional properties are attributed to things in order to explain their manifest dispositions: to explain how things will, or be likely to, behave in various kinds of circumstances. Such explanations are easily parodied, for they often appear to be trivial. The manifest disposition of takers of a given drug to go to sleep following its ingestion is only trivially explained by saying that the drug is a soporific. Nevertheless, this is a genuine explanation, and it is not the only possible one. The drug taker might believe the drug to be a soporific, when it is only a placebo, and the disposition to sleep might well be caused by this belief, rather than by the nature of the drug that is taken. The dispositional properties of things cannot, therefore, be defined behaviouristically, and ought not to be identified with the dispositions they are postulated to explain. The manifest, behaviouristically describable dispositions of things might have many different causes (as the case of the placebo soporific illustrates).

A natural kind of process that is a display of a given dispositional property has a real essence. In the case of any simple causal process, this real essence will be a dispositional property, and the scientific problem will be to specify precisely what this property is. The manifest dispositions of things are likely to be symptomatic of the processes in which they are involved, and often the best explanation of a disposition will be just that there is an underlying dispositional property that is directly responsible for it. But sometimes the best explanation will turn out to be much more complex. Perhaps several different kinds of processes are involved in producing the dispositions that are to be explained. The causal processes that are involved in the detailed explanation of a given disposition will all have the same kind of structure. Each will be characterizable by the kind (or kinds) of circumstance C that *would* trigger or initiate the action, and the kind (or kinds) of outcome(s) E that *would* (or would with probability p) result, *provided that there were no interfering or distorting influences*. The qualification is required because processes rarely occur in isolation, and what is actually observed will often be the combined effect of many different processes occurring simultaneously.

Real dispositional properties thus ground natural kinds of causal processes. But like all natural kinds, these natural kinds of causal processes exist independently of our systems of classification. Natural processes that appear to be of the same kind may turn out to be essentially different, and kinds of processes that appear to be very different may be just different species of the same kind. Refraction through a prism, and diffraction from a grating, produce very similar outcomes. Nevertheless, they are essentially different kinds of processes. One results from the refractivity of a medium, the other does not. On the other hand, many of the most important discoveries in science result from identifying apparently very different kinds of processes as species of the same generic kind. Newton, for example, showed that the apparently different kinds of processes of falling towards the earth and orbiting the sun are essentially the same. Similarly, Lavoisier showed that respiring, rusting and burning are all essentially processes of oxidation. Malcolm Forster (1988) talks of discovering a common cause in these and similar cases. But perhaps these discoveries would best be described as discoveries of sameness of essential nature.

Natural kinds of processes may be either causal or stochastic (i.e. probabilistic). An example of a natural kind of stochastic process is β-decay. β-decay is essentially the spontaneous emission of an electron from the nucleus of an atom resulting in an increase by one of its atomic number. It is a process that occurs independently of human concerns, and it has its own essential nature. To specify a kind of stochastic process such as this, it would appear to be sufficient to say what happens when it occurs, and how probable it is that it will occur within a given time interval. The properties responsible for stochastic processes generally are known as "propensities". But not all propensities are quite like β-decay, for there are other kinds of stochastic processes that do not occur spontaneously, but have to be triggered in some way. However, the focus of this book is not on propensities of either of these kinds, but rather on dispositional properties whose laws of action are deterministic, and that are, therefore, much more straightforwardly of the nature of causal powers.

The main difference between the analysis of dispositional properties that is proposed here and its more traditional rivals lies in the semantics of dispositional terms used to refer to them. Dispositional terms may be defined operationally by specifying the conditions for saying that something has, or does not have, a given disposition. But dispositional properties cannot be so defined. Dispositional properties, if they exist, have essential natures, and it is the business of natural science, not of semanticists, to discover and describe these natures. Consider the situation that existed before the chemical composition of water was known. At such a time, the term "water" might well have been defined in terms of the manifest characteristics of water. And this definition might have served reasonably well to pick out the same substance on each occasion of its use. But water is a natural kind of substance, and its essential nature could only be discovered by scientific investigation. When it was, and the essential nature of water then became known, any nominal definition of the term "water" would naturally have been superseded by the real definition of water as H_2O. The situation with dispositional terms and dispositional properties is similar. If a dispositional term reliably picks out the members of a natural kind of causal process, then there is a further question: what is the essential nature of this kind of process? It is then the job of natural science to describe the dispositional property that grounds processes of this kind. This is not a question that can be settled by appealing to the conventions of language, for real dispositional properties exist as distinct entities, prior to any nominalist or operationalist definitions of the terms we might use to refer to them.

This analysis of dispositions has some distinct advantages over more traditional theories. First, it explains why dispositions bear special relationships to subjunctive conditionals.[12] Dispositional properties support subjunctives because their existence entails that certain kinds of natural processes would occur in certain kinds of (possibly idealized) circumstances to the objects that have these properties. The subjunctive conditionals simply spell out these implications. Secondly, it explains why dispositional properties can be mocked or frustrated, for circumstances can often be manipulated to make an object appear to have a dispositional property that it does not have, or appear not to have a dispositional property that it does have. Thirdly, it explains why genuine dispositional properties can often be obscured. They can be obscured because different processes can occur in the same thing at the same time, so that the effect of any single dispositional property being triggered may well be obscured by the effects of other dispositional properties that are being simultaneously manifested.

An attractive feature of this analysis is that it leaves dispositional properties to be identified and explicated rather than defined operationally. And the process of explication is not philosophic, linguistic or lexicographic. It is a posteriori and scientific.

---

12. A subjunctive conditional is a conditional proposition (i.e. an "if . . . then . . ." proposition) in the subjunctive mood. It is thus a proposition that says what *would* happen if certain conditions *were to be* fulfilled, or what *would have* happened, if certain conditions *had been* fulfilled. Often such conditionals are asserted in the belief that the relevant conditions either have not been, or will not be, fulfilled.

CHAPTER 5

Laws of Nature

Introduction

According to A. R. Hall, the idea that nature is governed by laws does not appear to have existed in the ancient Greek, Roman or Far Eastern traditions of science. Hall suggests that the idea arose due to a "peculiar interaction between the religious, philosophic and legalistic ideas of the medieval European world".[13] There were probably other sources of the idea too. There were, for example, the influence of Euclid's geometry and Archimedes' statics in the medieval period in Europe, and the attempt that was then made to apply geometrical methods to the study of mechanics. These ancient works must have suggested to the medievals, as geometry had suggested to the ancient Greeks, that knowledge is structured. Moreover, the successes that were achieved in the early medieval period in solving problems of mechanical equilibrium, making use of such principles as the law of the lever, the principles of moments and virtual work, would certainly have added substance to the idea that nature is governed by laws.

Whatever may have been the origin of the concept of a law of nature, it is certainly true that the laws of nature were conceived from

---

13. Hall says:

> the concept of natural law in the social and moral senses familiar to medieval jurists, and ... [its employment in the phrase "laws of nature"] signifies a notable departure from the Greek attitude to nature. The use of the word "law" in such contexts would have been unintelligible in antiquity, whereas the Hebraic and Christian belief in a deity who was at once Creator and Law-giver rendered it valid. (1954: 172)

81

medieval times as general principles governing the kinds of motions that can be observed (kinematics), and the kinds of equilibrium states that can exist (statics). The modern concept of a law of nature is not so very different in conception, although it is no longer focused on laws of motion and equilibrium. The laws of nature are still widely thought of as principles *governing* nature – that is, as imposing order and structure upon it – but there are many other sciences than those that were known in medieval times, and many laws that do not fit neatly into the patterns of either kinematics or statics.

According to essentialists, the laws of nature describe the essences of the natural kinds. They are not prescriptive of how things should behave, but descriptive of how they must behave, given their essential natures. Any analysis of laws of nature must therefore begin with an analysis of the natural kinds. According to essentialists, natural kinds are fundamental to any account of the nature of reality, for, if they are right, then the world is wholly structured at the most fundamental levels into natural kinds, and the laws of nature are all determined by these kinds. The natural kinds, they say, exist in three, or perhaps four, different categories, and are related to each other within each category in the manner of species within a biological category. Therefore, they argue, the system of laws of nature must have a similar hierarchical structure.

The hierarchies of natural kinds

The natural kinds that exist in nature appear to be either natural kinds of objects or substances, natural kinds of events or processes, or natural kinds of facts about the intrinsic natures of things. Hence there should be laws of nature specific to each of these categories.

The category of objects or substances includes all of the chemical substances, all of the atoms and molecules of which they consist, the subatomic particles, and all of the material objects in the world that consist of any such ingredients. It is thus a wide-ranging category that includes every physical object or substance, from the tiniest of subatomic particles to the universe itself. The category of events and processes includes all of the physical processes that can or do take place in the world, including the process of continuing to exist unchanged, where this is possible. The category of events and processes is thus concerned with the dynamics of the world, and what can happen to things over time. This, too, is a very broad-ranging category, including processes occurring at all levels of existence, from the sub-microscopic to events like the Big Bang and the Hubble expansion of the universe. The third category of properties and structures is less obviously a single category, and, as we shall see, a good case can be made for splitting it in two. The properties of things include all of their causal powers, capacities and propensities: all of the things that they are disposed to do. These dispositional properties of things are not events or processes, however; nor are they objects or substances, as are the things that have these properties. If there is but a single category here, then it must also include all of the categorical properties that things can have. It must include the complex states of affairs that can exist in a region (e.g. as the circumstances in which a thing can exist). The category must also include the various ways in which fields can be structured (intrinsic structures), and the ways in which complex objects may be put together (block structures).

Within each of these categories there are natural hierarchies of natural kinds, with the natural kinds at the higher levels of generality including those at the lower levels as species. The category of objects or substances, for example, includes the natural kind that consists of all chemical compounds. And this natural kind includes the natural kind that consists of all halides, which in turn includes the natural kind that consists of all chlorides, which in turn includes the natural kind that is common salt. Similar hierarchies are to be found in the other categories. Thus, there are two very general kinds of processes occurring in nature: causal interactions and energy transfer processes. The causal interactions include those between particles (e.g. of the kind that may be observed in cloud chambers), and events of decay from higher to lower energy levels, including those of spectral emission and radioactive decay. As far as we know, these changes are all discontinuous and instantaneous. One state simply gives rise to another discretely different state, and there appears to be no transition from one to the other. The energy transfer processes, on the other hand, are essentially very different, for they are both continuous and temporally extended. The energy transfer processes all have at least these features:

- they are initiated and terminated by causal interactions
- they are inertial in the sense that they do not require any external forces or other external causal mechanisms to sustain them
- they are conservative of mass-energy, charge, spin, momentum, and all other universally conserved quantities (as indeed are the

causal interactions)

- if they transmit information concerning such quantities, then they do so at speeds not greater than that of light
- they are quantum-mechanically indeterminate; that is, they have no stages that are localized in space and time.

Most of the processes we think of as causal involve both causal interactions and inertial processes that communicate energy, momentum, charge and so on. Nevertheless, we may distinguish many natural kinds of causal processes, at various levels of generality. The chemical interactions, for example, are all natural kinds of processes. They are complex, and generally involve both elementary events – instantaneous changes of state – and energy transmission processes. But these complex kinds of processes satisfy all of the requirements for being considered to be natural kinds (see pp. 26–7). Indeed, if we know the chemical equation for a given chemical process, then we know its essential nature, for no other kind of process could have this same equation, and if any process is correctly described by this equation, then it must be a process of this chemical kind.

The *natural properties* of things are natural kinds of facts about them, but not just any old facts! They are *natural kinds of facts about the intrinsic natures of things*. The simplest kinds of natural properties refer to the most elementary of such facts. To illustrate: if something is 2 grams in mass, then the fact that this is so is an elementary fact about its intrinsic nature. If another thing is also 2 grams in mass, then this is an elementary fact about the intrinsic nature of this other thing. These two facts are evidently facts of the same kind, since they both are cases of things being 2 grams in mass. Moreover, this is a natural kind of elementary fact, since the kind exists independently of human knowledge and understanding, and is objective in the required sort of way. Therefore, we may identify the property of being 2 grams in mass with this natural kind of fact. The property of being 2 grams in mass is just the natural kind whose members are cases of things being 2 grams in mass. Philosophers call instances of such kinds of facts about the intrinsic natures of things "tropes" (as we saw in Chapter 3). Thus, if something has the property of being 2 grams in mass, then there is said to be a trope of this property in this particular thing.

A similar analysis applies to any other causal power, capacity or propensity, such as that of having a charge e, or of being water-soluble. The property of being water-soluble, for example, is the natural kind whose members are cases of substances being water-soluble. It also applies to structural properties. The property of being spherical, for example, is a natural kind whose members are all cases of things being spherical. The property of two things being two metres apart is a natural kind whose members are all cases of two things being two metres apart, and so on. Thus, the analysis is applicable whatever the nature of the property, and is satisfied both by dispositional properties (causal powers, etc.) and by categorical ones (structural properties). The existence of such a general analysis – one that is applicable to both dispositional and categorical properties – is a good reason for holding on to the idea that there is a single category that includes both.

As with the other two categories of natural kinds, there is a natural hierarchy of properties. The property of having mass, for example, is more general than that of having a mass of 2 grams, since everything that has a mass of 2 grams has mass, but not everything that has mass has a mass of 2 grams. The natural kind whose members are things having mass is therefore much more inclusive than the natural kind whose members are things having a mass of just 2 grams. The property of being an inertial force, on the other hand, is more general still, since this property includes moment of inertia (which measures a body's resistance to torque) as well as mass (which measures a body's resistance to linear forces). At still greater levels of generality we have the distinction between the categorical properties and dispositional ones. This appears to be a fundamental distinction, since the most general of the laws of categorical properties and structures – for example, those of general relativity – have the kind of scope that one naturally associates with global laws.

The hierarchies of laws of nature

For essentialists, the laws of nature are explications of the essential properties of the natural kinds. Therefore, if the natural kinds are divided into categories, as they suppose, and there are hierarchies within each of these categories, then we should expect to find that the laws of nature also divide naturally into these categories, and are structured hierarchically within each of them. The natural kinds of broadest scope in any given category must, of course, be inclusive of all of the other natural kinds that fall under them. But if the category is a unified one, then we should expect there to be a very general category-wide kind that includes all of the others. We should not expect these very general natural kinds to have names, because there are no other kinds of things of like category in the actual world with which to contrast them. But let us give them names, nevertheless, and call these very general kinds "world-objects", "world-processes" and "world-properties", according to their category. The laws concerning these most general kinds are those we recognize as global, since they cover all things within the category over which they range. The conservation laws, for example, are global in this sense, and it is a necessary truth that all world-processes are intrinsically conservative of each of the conserved quantities. Of course, there could be processes of a kind that are not intrinsically conservative of energy, or another conserved quantity. But these processes must be alien, and so not included in the category of world-processes. Therefore, if all world-processes are intrinsically conservative of energy, then this is not only true, but necessarily true.

The more specific laws in the broad category of events and processes include all of the causal or statistical laws of nature concerning the actions or interactions of things. These normally differ from each other in both scope and subject matter. The laws of energy transmission and of particle interactions are laws of this category. They are of intermediate generality. The laws of electromagnetic radiation, for example, and those of inertial motion are laws concerning ubiquitous natural kinds of processes, but they are not laws concerning all natural kinds of processes. The same is true of the laws of action of the various kinds of forces that exist in nature. They describe the actions of some, but not all, of the forces in nature. They are process laws, however, because they do describe the essential natures of the causal processes that must result from the actions of these forces. The laws of chemical action and interaction are likewise causal process laws, although they are more restricted still in their scope. They specifically describe the essences of the natural kinds of processes or interactions that are the subject matter of chemical investigation.

The most general laws in the category of objects are like those in the category of processes in that they hold necessarily of all things in the world in their category. There is one such law that comes immediately to mind, namely the principle of physicalism. According to this principle, every world-object is necessarily a physical object: an object that has energy, and is capable of interacting causally with other physical objects. The Cartesian thesis that there are two kinds of substances, mental and physical, is necessarily false, if the principle of physicalism is true. Another global law in the category of objects is the matter–anti-matter symmetry principle, according to which every kind of material particle has an anti-material counterpart, and conversely. The specific laws in this category are, of course, the laws describing the essential natures of the various kinds of objects that exist. The laws of chemical composition, therefore, are all laws of this kind, as are those describing the crystalline structures of various substances. However, the most fundamental laws in this area, apart from the global ones, are those describing the properties of the fundamental particles.

In the category of properties, we must include all of the dispositional properties of the various natural kinds of objects, as well as all of the intrinsic structural and block structural properties. Hence, any global laws in this category would have to be descriptive of the essential natures of all such properties. However, I know of no such laws. Perhaps this indicates that the category is too broad, and should be split up into sub-categories, for example, dispositional properties and structural properties. If we do split the category in this way, we can certainly pick out some very general principles in each of the sub-categories. There is, for example, a law of constant action for dispositional properties. The law states that the dispositional properties that exist all have constant laws of action of a certain kind. Specifically, for each dispositional property, there is a definite function (usually probabilistic) from the magnitude of the property, and the quantitative properties of the triggering circumstances, to the properties of the subsequent display. This display function is of the essence of the property, and the kind of process that it describes is a natural kind of process.

For the sub-category of structures, the most general laws are much more familiar, for all structures, whether intrinsic or block, are thought to be structures in a relativistic space-time of four dimensions. Hence the laws of general relativity may be considered to have the status of global laws in this sub-category. Some of the principles of quantum mechanics are also very general, and evidently apply to all kinds of intrinsic structures. Planck's law, for example, states a *general* equivalence between the energy of a thing and the frequency of the associated wave. Heisenberg's uncertainty principle and Pauli's exclusion principle impose certain *absolute* restrictions on the co-existence of states.

There are some good reasons, however, not to split the category of properties and structures into two sub-categories. First, it is possible to say generally what it is for anything to be a member of the category. Any fact about the intrinsic nature of a thing that is not just a conjunction, disjunction or negation of other facts is an instance of some property of that thing, whether it be a fact about its structure, or a fact about its causal powers, capacities or propensities. But secondly, and perhaps more importantly, there are many laws that appear to belong to both sub-categories. The laws of distribution of forces, such as Newton's law of gravity, appear to be both dispositional and structural. They describe how massive bodies are intrinsically disposed to act on each other, and, at the same time, they describe the structure of the Newtonian gravitational field. Of course, Newton's laws are no longer accepted. But the space–time–energy structure of general relativity is also a description of the causal powers of space-time.

Essentialists take the view that all of the laws of nature can thus be seen to be descriptive of the essential natures of the natural kinds that exist in the world. The global laws, they say, describe the essential natures of the category-wide kinds; the more specific laws describe the essential natures of the various species of things within these categories. If this is right, then there are two very important consequences. First, all of the laws of nature are metaphysically necessary, for it follows that they could not be other than they are in any world with the same ontology. The laws could not be otherwise, they say, because nothing could be a thing of the kind of which the law is essentially descriptive if it were not, or did not act, as the law provides. Secondly, the world is essentially as essentialists say it is, namely, a world whose laws are determined by its ontology, and not a passive world in which the laws are contingent, and superimposed on an already existing reality.

Desiderata for a theory of laws

Most philosophers would agree that laws of nature are not just accidental regularities. That is, they do not refer to regularities which just happen to hold, such as "All of the coins in my pocket are ten cent pieces". How then are they to be distinguished from them? The problem is usually posed as though it were a formal one of distinguishing two kinds of universal statements: nomic (law-like) and accidental (due to chance). In particular, it is asked, what are the distinguishing features of those universal generalizations that entitle them to be called laws of nature?

This way of posing the question assumes that laws of nature are really universal generalizations of some kind, and the problem is seen as being to specify the kind of generalization they are. However, this suggests a much closer link between accidental and nomic universals than most essentialists would be prepared to admit. The laws of nature, they claim, are descriptions of the essences of natural kinds, and so must hold **for** all possible members of the kinds they describe. Law-statements are therefore fundamentally concerned with what *must be* the case, and not merely with what *is* the case. Accidental generalizations, on the other hand, are never concerned with anything other than what is the case.

But let us not beg the question of the character of the laws of nature. Let us start from what is common to all accounts. First, it is generally agreed that the laws of nature are fundamentally universal propositions of some kind, that is, that they are universal in form. In the simplest cases, they refer to all of the members of some class, and say something that is true of all of them. That is, they have the form "All As are Bs". In more complex cases, the laws may range over a number of different classes, describing the properties of, and the relationships that may hold between, things in these classes, and describing what they would do in these various circumstances. Propositions of this nature are multiply universal in form, but not essentially very different. Secondly, it is generally agreed that the reference classes may not be restricted to known cases, or limited spatially or temporally, for laws are required to be explanatory, and provide a basis for making predictions. Propositions that are epistemically, or spatially or temporally restricted would not be satisfactory for this purpose, and so not eligible to be classed as laws of nature.

This is all more or less common ground. It is also widely, although not universally, accepted that the laws of nature are in some sense necessary. That is, it is not just an accident that things obey these laws, but there is a sense in which they must do so. The laws of nature must be able to support hypothetical reasoning, that is, they must make it possible for us to say what *would* happen if things were other than they are. Thus all causal explanations depend on our being able to contrast what actually occurs with what would occur in other possible (but not actual) circumstances. Therefore, for causal explanation to be possible, we must be able to say what would, or would not, happen in conditions other than those that actually prevail. The laws of nature are required to tell us this. In philosophers' jargon, *they must support counter-factual conditionals*. Thus, if it is a law that all As are Bs, then not only must all As be Bs, but it must also be the case that if anything else were to be an A, then it too would have to be a B. Such knowledge is indispensable to scientific explanation, and depends on our knowing that some things are not only true, but necessarily true.

Although it is widely accepted that the laws of nature must have a kind of necessity, there is no such agreement about the nature of this necessity – other than of its capacity to support counter-factual or hypothetical reasoning. The laws of nature have had to be discovered empirically. So it is initially implausible to suppose that they are analytic, or formally logically necessary. It is commonly supposed, therefore, that laws of nature are necessary in some weaker sense of "necessity". But what could this be? Presumably, the laws of nature are physically necessary. But then, how is physical necessity to be defined? Manifestly, it will not do to say that the physically necessary propositions are just those that are true in all worlds governed by the same laws as ours, for this would be to argue in a circle. One might as well try to define a historically necessary proposition as any that is true in all worlds with the same history as ours.

The first desideratum for a theory of laws, then, is that it should give an adequate account of their peculiar necessity. This is the "necessity problem". Van Fraassen (1989) draws attention to the difficulty of giving an adequate account of what he calls "natural necessity". However, as he construes the problem, it is that of identifying the relationship in virtue of which an empirical generalization acquires the status of a law of nature. Accordingly, he calls this difficulty the "problem of identification". However, in so construing the problem, he begs an important question, for his way of posing it presupposes that natural necessitation is a relation that somehow *imparts* its character to what would otherwise be just an ordinary empirical generalization. This presupposition must be rejected. Natural necessity is not like greatness; laws of nature do not achieve necessity, or have necessity thrust upon them – they just are that way.[14]

One common and important property of laws that has received very little attention in the philosophical literature is their abstract or idealized nature. There are very few laws that apply directly to the kinds of things or processes that are actually observable in the world, and those that do are generally regarded as low-level empirical

---

14. With apologies to Shakespeare: "some men are born great, some achieve greatness, and some have greatness thrust upon them" (*Twelfth Night*, II, iv, 158).

generalizations. Most of the propositions we think of as being (or as expressing) genuine laws of nature seem to describe only the behaviour of ideal kinds of things, or of things in ideal circumstances. This common feature of laws has often been noted, but most theories of laws do little or nothing to explain it. Many writers have supposed that the fact that idealizations occur in so many laws reflects only our need to simplify nature in order to understand it.[15] Nature is too complex, it is said, for us to be able to formulate basic laws that apply directly to it. Our laws are therefore a kind of compromise between truth and intelligibility. As statements about reality, they are at best only approximations to the truth.

This account of idealization in science is unsatisfactory. It does not explain why highly idealized theoretical models should often be preferred. Moreover, they are evidently preferred *even when more realistic models are available*. (Think of black body radiators and perfectly reversible heat engines.) There is therefore an "idealization problem". In meteorological and economic forecasting, accuracy of prediction is important, if not always achievable. Consequently, to the extent that economic and meteorological models do not accurately reflect reality, they are unsatisfactory. In these fields, therefore, our theoretical models are expected to be *as realistic as possible*. But weather and economic forecasting are not typical sciences. Typically, the emphasis in science is not on forecasting, but on *understanding*. And, for reasons that are not well understood, this often seems to require high levels of abstraction and idealization, and the construction of models that are known to be unrealistic.

Another property that any decent theory of laws should be able to account for is their objectivity. That is, the laws of nature should be *discoverable*, and therefore be or describe some reality that exists independently of us. This is so, I think, even if it can be argued that there are conventional elements in some of the laws we accept, for the laws of nature are clearly not just *inventions*, or abstract mathematical constructions. Many of them, at least, are postulates about the structure of reality or the kinds of processes that can occur in nature. This being so, we should be able to say precisely what features of reality the laws of nature describe. This would be straightforward enough, if a Humean regularity theory of laws were defensible, and the necessity of laws could be adequately accounted for independently of their descriptive roles. Then their basis in reality would be just the universal

---

15. See, for example, Scriven (1961).

regularities they describe. However, a Humean theory of laws is not defensible, and the usual accounts of natural necessity are unsatisfactory. But, if a Humean regularity theory is rejected, then there is a problem concerning the ontological foundations of laws: in what features of reality are the laws of nature grounded? This is the "ontological problem".

It seems, then, that there are at least three major problems about laws of nature: a necessity problem, an idealization problem and an ontological problem. Any adequate theory of laws should yield satisfying solutions to all of these. Also, as we have seen, there are several different categories of laws of nature, and within each category there is a hierarchy. A good theory of laws of nature should do something to explain this structure. Therefore we may add one more important problem to the list: the "structural problem".

Currently accepted theories of laws are not satisfactory on all counts. Humean regularity theories do not provide acceptable solutions to the necessity or idealization problems, since they are unable to explain the necessity of laws, and they cannot account for their often idealized character. Conventionalist theories of laws, such as those developed by the positivists in the first few decades of the twentieth century, fare better with the necessity and idealization problems, but fail to provide a satisfying ontology of laws. They do not explain the objectivity of laws of nature, because they do not explain how the laws of nature are grounded in reality. The natural necessitation theories that have been developed in the past twenty years or so seem promising for dealing with the ontological problem. But it is now becoming increasingly clear that the only kind of theory of laws of nature that is capable of solving both the necessity and ontological problems is an essentialist one: a theory on which the basic laws of nature are held to be metaphysically necessary. The essentialist theory also throws new light on the idealization problem. Finally, no theory of laws, other than the essentialist one, does much to resolve the structural problem.

The regularity theory of laws

According to Hume, the laws of nature are causal laws, and causal laws are just regularities of some kind. They are not necessary, except in the sense that they are *felt* by us to be so. From the appearance of the cause, we may come, by habit-forming experience, to anticipate the effect. So the effect naturally seems to us to be produced by the cause, and so necessitated by it. But, according to Hume, the supposed "production" or "necessitation" of the effect is really just an illusion that is created by our anticipation of it. It does not exist in reality.

Many philosophers who are otherwise sympathetic to Hume's philosophy have not been happy with Hume's account of natural necessity, that is, the sort of necessity that is supposed to characterize causal laws. To say that one kind of event, say A, is the cause of another, say B, is not just to say that whenever an A occurs a B will occur, for this might be true just by chance. For one thing to be the cause of another, it is argued, it must in some sense *bring it about*, so that if circumstances of the kind A were to recur, an event of the kind B *would then have to* occur. But a Humean, it seems, cannot have the required concept of causal power, because, from a Humean perspective, there is no such thing as a necessary connection between events that is conceivable by us.[16]

Humean theories of laws also have trouble with the idealization problem. What can a Humean say about the law L that states that the efficiency of any perfectly reversible heat engine working between temperature limits t_1 and t_2 is the same, and is greater than that of any irreversible heat engine working between these same temperature limits? Considered as a universal generalization it is vacuously true (in the sense explained in note 2, p. 15). In practice, it is not possible to build a heat engine that comes even close to being perfectly reversible, and the efficiencies of real heat engines are a long way below their theoretical maxima. A Humean might try the suggestion that L is not really a law, but a definition. However, it does not appear to be a definition of perfect reversibility, or of efficiency, or of any of the other terms used in its statement. Perhaps, then, it is like a proposition of Euclidean geometry. Perhaps. But then, a Humean is obliged to deny that L is a law of nature, for the laws of nature are supposed to be regularities of some kind, and not theorems of abstract theoretical systems.

One common Humean strategy for dealing with the idealization problem is to argue that ideal laws, like L, are really compromises between the competing demands of accuracy and comprehensibility. The true laws, which apply directly to reality, would often be far too

---

16. Against this, Fales (1990) argues, persuasively in my view, that forces of the sort required to explain causal connections *are* conceivable by us. Our concept of causation, he says, derives from our experience of *bodily force* (pp. 11–25). Thus, Fales confronts, head on, Hume's "inconceivability" objection to the claim that there are causal powers in nature (pp. 25–39).

complicated to be stated in an intelligible way. Therefore, we must make simplifying assumptions, and make do with approximations that we can grasp and work with. This is the so-called "approximation defence". However, there are many good reasons for thinking that this is not the motivation for idealization in science.

First, ideal laws often remain the fundamental ones, even when much more realistic laws are known. The perfect gas laws, for example, are still the fundamental laws of the theory of gases, even though real gases are not perfect, and are known to behave in other ways, more or less as Van der Waals's equation of state implies. However, the theory of perfect gases remains the basic theory, and Van der Waals's equation of state is just a modification of it that is of no great theoretical interest. It is not that Van der Waals's equation is very complex. On the contrary, it is quite simple. Van der Waals's equation is not discussed very much in physics textbooks, simply because it is not very interesting. Secondly, even some of the most fundamental laws of nature are abstract. The conservation laws, for example, all refer to idealized systems. These laws are supposed to hold exactly only for systems that are closed and isolated. They are not thought to hold precisely for the kinds of open and interacting systems we find in nature. Therefore, a Humean who adopts the approximation defence is obliged to say that these laws too are a compromise between the demands of accuracy and comprehensibility. This is surely nonsense. These are the fundamental laws of nature, and not approximations to the true laws adopted as a kind of compromise.

Of course, the universe itself is a closed and isolated system, so it cannot be said that the conservation laws are all vacuously true. But the conservation laws also tell us a great deal about what happens locally, and would be almost useless if they did not do so. Therefore, any satisfactory account of the laws of nature must deal adequately with the idealization problem, which is raised in a very acute form by the conservation laws. The fact that the conservation laws all apply globally is not much of a consolation to a Humean. The regularity theorist must be able to explain how the conservation laws can apply locally, *even though none of the open and interactive systems we find in nature actually obeys them*.[17]

Another possible line of defence for a Humean would be to argue that the idealized laws we find in science express deep regularities:

---

17. This is the problem Bhaskar (1978) focused on in his critique of the Humean theory of science.

regularities that may never, or very rarely, appear at the surface level. But, if a Humean takes this view, he or she immediately runs into difficulties with the ontological problem, for what are the idealized objects involved in these deep regularities? Are there really, deep down, closed and isolated systems, inertial frames, perfectly reversible heat engines, and the like? If not, then how can these deep regularities exist?

Conventionalist theories of laws

At the turn of the nineteenth century, Henri Poincaré, and a number of philosophers, most notably Ernst Mach, defended the view that many of the most fundamental laws of nature are not just empirical generalizations, as Hume had supposed, but conventions adopted because of their convenience in organizing and systematizing experience. The experimentally discovered laws that our theories are designed to explain were, of course, held to be empirical generalizations. But many of the *basic* laws of nature that are embedded in our explanatory theories were held to have a different status. These laws cannot be verified or refuted experimentally, it was held, for the simple reason that they are *not* experimental laws. They are *conventions* adopted because of their utility as components of theories. Consequently, they would cease to be accepted only if they ceased to be useful for this purpose, or if more useful conventions could be proposed to take their place. Laws of nature having the status of conventions might stand or fall with the theoretical structure that they support, but not independently of it.

According to Mach and Poincaré, the laws of nature have a status similar to that of a geometrical theorem. They would say, for example, that the law of inertia is true in Newtonian mechanics (since it is an axiom of that system), just as they would say that Playfair's axiom is true in Euclidean geometry. They would not say of either axiom that it is true absolutely, since other geometries and other systems of mechanics can be developed to describe the same reality. The laws of mechanics, like the laws of geometry, are conventional.

This conventionalist theory of laws gains plausibility and support from the fact that many laws, especially many of the most fundamental laws, apply strictly only to ideal systems existing in various kinds of ideal circumstances, for such laws can easily be construed as conventions. Conventionalists would say, for example, that the law of conservation of energy is a convention – one that serves (at least partly) to define the concept of a closed and isolated system. Therefore, they would say, there cannot be any exceptions to the law of conservation of energy. If we come across a system for which energy is not conserved, then this only shows that it is either not closed or not isolated.

As a theory of laws of nature, conventionalism has some good things to be said for it. First, it accounts well for the necessity of many basic laws. These laws, they say, are necessary, simply because they are true by definition or convention. On the other hand, since we have to discover, presumably by trial and error, what conventions are best for our theoretical purposes, what conventions should be adopted is partly an empirical question. So conventionalists were easily able to account for the necessity of the fundamental laws, and also for their a posteriori, or empirical, character. Moreover, since, according to conventionalism, the conventions we adopt must be chosen specifically for the purposes of theory construction, they can continue to be accepted only if they continue to be useful for this purpose. If the theory is superseded by a better theory in which other, more useful, conventions are adopted, then the laws might be considered to have been falsified (although, strictly speaking, they have just become obsolete).

Secondly, conventionalism accounts well for the abstractness and ideality of certain laws, for if the laws of nature have a status similar to geometrical theorems, as conventionalists maintain, then they must be concerned with abstract, idealized entities similar to those of geometry. They cannot be concerned directly with real objects or processes, conventionalists say, for then they would be open to empirical refutation. And, if the axioms or theorems of a physical theory were empirically testable, then they would not have the status of axioms. What is testable, according to conventionalism, is only whether the theory can be applied as it was intended to be.

So it looks as though conventionalists can deal well with both the necessity and the idealization problems. The laws are necessary, conventionalists say, because they have the status of theorems in an abstract theoretical system, and they are idealized for just this same reason. However, the causal laws of physical and chemical systems are manifestly not just theorems in an abstract theoretical structure. The laws of chemical composition and chemical interaction, for example, are not abstract theorems, but laws about substances and their behaviour. All attempts to construe them otherwise have been lamentable failures. There are still some conventionalists who, like Duhem almost a century ago, think of chemical theory as an abstract logical structure, rather than as a body of theory that is descriptive of the underlying chemical reality. But these theorists are finding their position increasingly difficult to maintain. If conventionalism requires the rejection of scientific realism, as it apparently does, then this is much too heavy a price to pay.

There is also trouble for conventionalism in its home territory, namely in the fields of gravitation, relativity and quantum mechanics, for conventionalists can offer no satisfactory account of why some "conventions" are so successful, and so much better than others. If the structural laws of nature are just conventions, how can we explain the fact that (with very few exceptions) there are often no viable alternatives to the conventions we have adopted? We can argue abstractly that logically distinct, but empirically equivalent, theories based on different conventions are always possible. However, viable alternatives that do not piggy-back on existing theories are hard to find. It is easy enough to construct an alternative theory T′ to any given theory T, if piggy-backing is allowed. For example, we might define T′ as any theory that is (a) incompatible with T, but (b) has the same empirical consequences as T. However, T′ is not a genuine alternative to T. It is a monster.

Moreover, even if T′ is allowed to count as a genuine alternative to T, there is still the question of why some conventions are manifestly so much better than others. Surely there must be some underlying reality to which a theory may, or may not, correspond that would explain this fact. Essentialists explain it by appealing to the natural kinds of things or structures existing in the world, which, they suppose, the laws describe. But conventionalists cannot explain the fact in the same way, since they cannot assume that their theories are descriptive of any such reality. The conventionalist theory of laws thus fails to provide a satisfactory resolution to the ontological problem.

Natural necessitation theories

As a result of the failure of Humean and conventionalist theories of laws to deal adequately with the problem of natural necessity, many philosophers have sought a more realistic basis for this kind of necessity. On any satisfactory theory, it is argued, the laws of nature must turn out to be necessarily true in virtue of some real relation of natural necessitation. Let us call any such theory a "natural necessitation theory". The new essentialist theory of laws is one such theory.

However, it is not the only one. In recent years, a number of philosophers have attempted to develop natural necessitation theories that will account for the necessity of laws, and yet, at the same time, preserve the intuition that the things that exist in the world could be governed by different laws of nature. Let us call any such theory a "contingent natural necessitation theory". Those who accept such a theory are forced to defend both the contingency and the necessity of laws, and consequently, they must, in the end, try to defend the view that natural necessity is a kind of hybrid between contingency and necessity. The laws of nature, they are forced to conclude, must, in some sense, or at some level, be contingent, while in another sense, or at another level, they are necessary.

Perhaps the best known theories of contingent natural necessitation are those due to Fred Dretske, Michael Tooley, David Armstrong and John Carroll. According to these theorists, and others who have followed them, there are various contingent relations between properties. It so happens, for example, that the property of being an electron (if, indeed this is a property rather than a natural kind) includes that of having negative charge e. In other worlds, however, the property of being an electron might not include that of having negative charge e. Consequently, it is not a necessary proposition – that is, one that is true in all possible worlds – that electrons have such a charge. Hence the law that all electrons have charge e is contingent. It is true in some worlds, but false in others. On the other hand, every electron in this world must have charge e, because of the inclusion relation that happens to hold between these two properties. So if any new electron is created in this world, then it too must have charge e, because, given that this inclusion relation exists, there could not possibly be an electron in this world that does not have this charge.

The supposed relationship between the properties (being an electron, and having charge e) thus guarantees the universality of the connection. For, if the relationship exists, then every electron in this world has charge e. The theory also does something to explain the necessity of the law. That is, if the relationship holds, then being an electron in this world must, in some sense, *necessitate* it having charge e, for it could not be an electron in this world if it did not have such a charge. Moreover, the theory achieves all this without commitment to any stronger kind of necessity for laws, for the necessity required is one of only contingent necessity, since it is one that depends on the relationship of inclusion holding in this world, which, by hypothesis, it might not do. In other worlds, perhaps, it does not hold, and there are electrons there that do not have charge *e*.

To many philosophers this has seemed like sleight of hand. The concept of a contingent necessity is an oxymoron, they say, because whatever is contingent is not necessary, for surely "contingent" just means "neither necessary nor impossible". This, at least, was my own initial reaction to the contingent natural necessitation thesis. However, I now see that there is much to be said in its favour. The supposed contingent relation between properties provides a metaphysical backing for a thesis of strict universality. And a strict universal with metaphysical backing is certainly more law-like than a strict universal without any such backing. If, in this world, being an A includes being a B, then, in this world, every A *must be* a B. The metaphysical relationship that is supposed to hold between these two properties guarantees the truth of the universal proposition. But if, in this world, being an A does not include being a B, then, while it may still be the case that every A is a B, this could only be so accidentally, or by chance. So the metaphysical backing does make a difference to the status of the proposition. If one thinks that a given universal generalization, "All As are Bs", does have this metaphysical backing, then one must accept it as a law of nature that all As are Bs. But if one thinks that it does not have this backing, then one must consider it to be no better than accidentally true that all As are Bs.

Against this, it will be argued that the supposed metaphysical backing makes no difference. If it is not a necessary truth that all As are Bs, then one cannot infer that if anything, say X, were to be or become an A, then it would have to be or become a B. This is true. However, such a proposition may nevertheless be assertible. And, for reasons we shall go into later (Chapter 7, pp. 130–34), what is assertible in hypothetical reasoning is what is important. The proposition that if X were to be or become an A, then it would have to become a B, will always be assertible if being an A is believed to include being a B, and X's being or becoming an A is not known to be impossible, for the guarantee provided by the metaphysical backing extends to any A that might exist, or might have existed, in this world. Therefore, it does make a difference whether or not one thinks that a generalization is backed by a relationship of natural necessitation between properties. If one thinks it has such a backing, then one will reason with it hypothetically as one would with a law of nature. But if one thinks it lacks any such backing, then one would not be epistemically justified in reasoning with it in this way.

The main difficulty with contingent natural necessitation theories is that they are just too contrived. Real properties are supposedly the same in all worlds in which they exist. They are what philosophers call "universals". But if the universals are the same in the different possible worlds, how can the relationships between them possibly be different in different possible worlds? How can the universal "being an electron" include "having charge *e*" in one world but not in another? This is a mystery that the defenders of the contingent natural necessitation thesis have never been able to explain. It is not absurd to suppose that there is a relation of natural necessitation holding between some pairs of properties and not between others. But it is, *prima facie*, absurd to suppose that this relationship holds between two properties in one world, but not between the same two properties in another world. Surely the relation of natural necessitation would have to be different in the different cases. How can A bear the relationship R to B in one world but not in another, if A, B and R are all the same?

The main trouble with contingent natural necessitation theories is that they seek to combine what is basically an Aristotelian theory of natural necessity with a Humean contingency thesis about laws. It cannot be done. There is no possible account of natural necessity that is compatible with the view that the laws of nature, and hence the law-making relation, is contingent. The problem of reconciling real relations of natural necessitation with a Humean metaphysic has not been, and cannot be, solved. If the relation between the universals is contingent, then the laws are contingent; if it is logically or meta-physically necessary, then the laws are logically or metaphysically necessary. If the relation of natural necessitation is some other kind of necessitation relation, then we are owed an account of it. It seems that no amount of metaphysical manoeuvring will escape this difficulty. What is needed is something more radical: a thoroughly non-Humean theory of natural necessitation.

The essentialist theory of laws of nature

The essentialist theory of laws of nature is one such radical alternative, for essentialists believe that the natural necessitation relations, on which the laws of nature all depend, are not contingent, but necessary. If being an A necessitates being a B in this world, they argue, then it does so in every world. Consequently, the laws of nature must themselves be necessary. There can be no question of a law of nature holding in one world, but not in another. If it is a law of nature, then it relates universals, and does so without reference to any particular worlds in which they might be instantiated. And the only kinds of relations between universals that there can be of this nature are necessary relations. To give substance to their view, essentialists claim that the laws of nature spell out the essential properties of the natural kinds. The natural necessitation relations, on which the laws of nature all depend, are thus to be identified with the relations that must hold between the natural kinds and their essential properties.

Essentialists argue, therefore, that the contingent natural necessitation theorists are right in at least one respect. The laws of nature do concern relations between universals, since natural kinds are a species of universals. The natural kinds may not all be universals as this term has traditionally been understood. But genuine properties and structures certainly are universals, even in the traditional sense, and natural kinds of objects and processes are formally just like properties or structures, except that they range over different kinds of things. Properties and structures are natural kinds of facts about the intrinsic natures of things; substantive and dynamic natural kinds refer to kinds of objects or substances, or to kinds of events and processes.

The essentialist theory of laws of nature seems to have decisive advantages over all other theories of laws. First, it explains the varieties and hierarchies of laws of nature in a simple and straightforward way. The hierarchies of natural kinds naturally give rise to corresponding hierarchies of laws, with global laws at their summits. Secondly, it explains the necessity of laws, since, according to essentialism, the laws of nature are all metaphysically necessary. That is, they are all true in every possible world.[18] Thirdly, it enables us to give a good account of the abstractness, or ideality, of many laws of nature, because the essential properties of things are necessarily to be found among their intrinsic properties, and the intrinsic properties of things are just those of its properties that it has independently of its causal relations to other things. Therefore, in order to describe the essential properties of anything, it is necessary to abstract from any external forces that may be acting upon it to say how it would be or behave in the absence of such forces. Fourthly, the essentialist theory provides a clear answer to the question: in virtue of what is a law of

18. Although, of course, they would only be vacuously true in worlds in which the relevant natural kinds did not exist.

nature true? The essentialist's reply is that laws of nature refer to the essential properties of the natural kinds, and that these are their truth-makers.

The main worry about the essentialist theory of laws is likely to concern the claim that the laws of nature are all metaphysically necessary. Many philosophers will agree that the laws of nature are necessary in some sense. But the claim that they are all metaphysically necessary will strike many as being far too strong. Surely the contingent natural necessitation theorists are right to look for something weaker – for a sense of necessity that is weaker than metaphysical necessity, but stronger than mere accidental universality. This issue will be taken up in Chapter 6.

Natural Necessity

Causal necessity

Hume's treatment of the problem of natural necessity dealt mainly with the relationship between cause and effect. He argued that all reasoning concerning matters of fact is ultimately founded on this relationship. So, he thought, the more general problem of justifying all sound reasoning of this kind could be solved if the more specific one of justifying reasoning from cause to effect could be. What then, he asked, is there about this relationship to justify such an inference? Is there, perhaps, some kind of necessary connection between causes and effects?

On this question we have conflicting intuitions. On the one hand, it seems obvious that the things we do and the events that occur in nature have effects, and that these effects are somehow *produced,* or *brought about,* by these actions and events. The effects would seem to be not just *subsequent happenings*, but, in most cases, *inevitable consequences* of the actions or events that give rise to them. On the other hand, the effects that are produced do not seem to be necessitated by their causes in the strong logical sense in which, say, adding one to an even number produces an odd number, because the contrary of any cause and effect relation is easily imaginable, "as if ever so conformable to reality" (Hume 1777: 21). Therefore, if causes necessitate their effects, then they must do so in some weaker, non-logical, sense.

But then, Hume asked, what is the foundation in experience of this idea of necessitation, or necessary connection, between events? What is its source? He examined a number of specific cases of causation in a mock attempt to find it, and concluded that there is nothing whatever in any of these cases, considered one at a time, to suggest the idea of necessary connection. So, in the following very famous passage, he concluded:

> upon the whole, there appears not, throughout all nature, any one instance of connexion which is conceivable by us. All events seem entirely loose and separate. One event follows another; but we never can observe any tie between them. They seem *conjoined*, but never *connected*. And as we can have no idea of any thing which never appeared to our outward sense or inward sentiment, the necessary conclusion *seems* to be that we have no idea of connexion or power at all, and that these words are absolutely without any meaning, when employed either in philosophical reasonings or common life.
>
> (Hume 1777: 74, original emphasis)

Hume did not accept this sceptical conclusion, however, for he went on to say that while there is nothing in any one experience that suggests the idea of a necessary connection, there is a source of this idea in repeated experiences, because repeated observations of instances of causal sequences may produce associations of ideas that determine our expectations about any new cases that we may come across. So it must be *repetition* that gives rise to the idea of necessary connections in nature. Therefore, in the world itself, Hume argued, there are no necessary connections, just regularities of various kinds.

Nearly everyone agrees that Hume's account of causal necessity will not do. It is difficult sometimes to put one's finger on mistakes in philosophical reasoning, and generations of philosophy students have wrestled with this particular problem. But, in this case, the mistake is fairly clearly in the premises. If you grant Hume his assumptions about reality, and what information we can gather as observers, his conclusions would seem to follow. But Hume's assumptions about the world and his role as an observer are quite unrealistic, because there is a big difference between being a detached and passive observer of the world and an active participant in it, and Hume's arguments all depend on the assumption that we are passive observers. Thus, he sees himself as a spectator watching and contemplating a sort of three-dimensional picture show, looking at a billiard table, for example, and trying to draw conclusions from what he sees. In this show, there are images of things moving around, apparently colliding with each other, or bouncing off each other, and seeming to do all of the things that ordinary things can be seen to do. But if this is how we experience reality, then there is indeed a serious problem about causal connections. What reason could we have for believing that one motion or change gives rise to another? Looked at this way, "all events seem loose and separate", as Hume himself said.

But now think of yourself as an active participant in the world, digging in the garden, starting the motor mower, being buffeted by the wind, getting wet in the rain, chopping down a tree, being hit by a falling branch, wheeling a barrow and so on. Then events no longer seem so loose and separate. On the contrary, one is constantly causing things to happen, and being affected by them, either in reaction, or independently. There are exertions, feelings of strain, pressures and felt impacts. With this image of oneself in the world, Hume's argument cannot get off the ground, for what is the basis in experience of the idea of causing something to happen, or being affected by something? The answer is obvious. It is the experience of doing things, or of having them done to you. The idea that it must be derivable from the experience of passively observing a passive reality, if it is to have any claim to legitimacy, is untenable. We are in the world, and manifestly interacting with it. So the origin of our concept of cause is not really a mystery. It can seem mysterious only if one starts out with a Humean conception of reality, and conceives oneself to be a detached and passive observer of it. Then, indeed, it is hard to make much sense of the idea that there are genuine causal connections in nature.

Essentialists take the view that we are active participants in the world, doing things, and having things done to us. Consequently, they have no difficulty in countering Hume's argument that causation is, in reality, nothing more than a species of regularity in the ways that things behave. The primary experiences that are the sources of our ideas of cause and effect are obvious enough to anyone who accepts the essentialist's point of view. Moreover, they are experiences that are graded and varied. Some effects require more effort to produce, or the efforts of several people combined. Some effects are greater than others, or greater in some directions than in others, and there are all sorts of correlations between causes and effects, many of which are obvious to us. Some things are more affected by causal influences than others, or more affected in some ways, and less affected in others. Consequently, our experience of living in the world, and interacting with it, gives rise to the idea that we have various causal powers, and that there are various causal powers in nature to which we, and other things, are constantly reacting. Moreover, it is clear that these causal powers can differ from each other in the kinds of effects they are able to bring about, in the circumstances of their production and in the magnitudes of their effects. So, for an essentialist, causation is not essentially an illusion resulting from habits of thought, as it is for a Humean. There are genuine causal powers in nature of greater or less strength, acting on various kinds of things, and producing many different kinds of effects.

Hume's argument is based on the premise that our passive observations of the world are primary, and that, to the extent that our understanding of the world is justified, it is based wholly on such observations. Essentialists deny this premise. For any essentialist, our experience of being in the world, as participants in its various processes, is primary. The capacity to stand back from the world to view it as a passing parade is not primitive, but highly sophisticated, for it is the capacity to abstract from all of the causal influences that we know about, in order to consider the world afresh, as if viewing it for the first time. Most people naturally have some difficulty with this, for it is not how we normally see the world, but how we must learn to see the world, if we are to appreciate the force of Hume's argument. Moreover, Hume's argument not only requires us to view the world as a passing parade, but to view it as a passive observer. Then, having thus prepared us, Hume drops his bombshell, asking "What is the source of our knowledge of cause and effect?" And the answer is, of course, that from such a standpoint we can have no knowledge of cause and effect. As passive observers we may be able to detect regularities of various kinds, and perhaps we could pick out a species of such regularities and label them "causal laws", but really they would just be regularities, and nothing more. However, we are not passive observers of the world; and the world is not just the object of our contemplation. The world is what we have to wrestle with.

Kant on a priori and empirical knowledge

In his *Critique of Pure Reason*, Kant makes the important distinction between a priori and a posteriori knowledge. A posteriori knowledge is knowledge that is derived from experience, either directly, by observation or introspection, or indirectly, by inference, ultimately from something that is known in such a way. A priori knowledge is knowledge that we have independently of experience. Kant offers the following two criteria for distinguishing between them:

> Experience teaches us that a thing is so and so, but not that it cannot be otherwise. First, then, if we have a proposition which in being thought is thought as *necessary*, it is an *a priori* judgement. Secondly, experience never confers on its judgements true or strict, but only assumed or comparative *universality*, through induction. We can properly only say, therefore, that, so far as we have hitherto observed, there is no exception to this or that rule.
>
> (Kant 1787: B3–4, original emphasis)

So, according to Kant, if any proposition is necessary or strictly universal, then it is an a priori judgement. If it is an a posteriori or empirical judgement, then it is neither necessary nor strictly universal.

As is well known, Kant makes a further distinction between *analytic* and *synthetic* judgements. Kant's original distinction could be applied directly only to universal affirmative statements, that is, judgements of the form "All As are Bs". A judgement is analytic, he said, if the subject concept A includes the predicate concept B, so that nothing is really added by it. A judgement is synthetic, on the other hand, if the concept B lies outside the concept A, so that in asserting that all As are Bs, something is added to the conception of it being an A. Nowadays, we would express the distinction a little more generally. A judgement is analytic, we would now say, if it is true just in virtue of the meanings of words.

Kant considered all analytic judgements to be a priori. It is true that we have to know the meanings of the relevant words to understand what such judgements are saying, but once we know the meanings of these words, we know all we need to know to make the judgement. No empirical investigation is needed to establish its truth. Indeed, if we did not already know its truth, we could make no empirical investigations at all concerning its subject matter. The standard example of an analytic judgement is "A bachelor is an unmarried man." This is analytic, it is said, because the concept of being a bachelor includes that of being an unmarried man. It is a priori, because it has the requisite necessity and universality. There can be no concern that we might one day come across a bachelor who is married, or is not a man. There could not be such a person.

Notoriously, Kant went on to argue that there are other judgements that are both synthetic and a priori, and Kant's great *Critique of Pure Reason* was his attempt to explain the nature of such judgements, and how they are possible. This was a major problem for Kant, because, as he saw it, the theorems of arithmetic, geometry and pure mechanics (the dominant science of his day) are either analytic (if true by definition) or synthetic a priori (if an axiom or theorem of the system). They are a priori, he argued, since they have the required necessity and universality, but they are synthetic because their truth is not derivable just by conceptual analysis.

Many philosophers have questioned whether Kant's category of synthetic a priori truths exists. According to the empiricist philosophers of the nineteenth and twentieth centuries, there are no such propositions. According to some (e.g. J. S. Mill), the propositions of arithmetic and geometry are very general empirical truths about the world, and indubitable only because they are evidently confirmed by the whole of our experience. According to others (e.g. David Hilbert), standard arithmetic and Euclidean geometry are just two of a number of purely formal deductive systems that tell us nothing whatever about the world, and their theorems are true only in the sense that they are derivable within these systems. According to other philosophers (e.g. Gottlob Frege), the propositions of arithmetic, and ultimately of other branches of mathematics, are all reducible to formal logical truths, and are therefore devoid of all factual content. As for the propositions of Newtonian mechanics, they were generally considered to be either very general empirical truths about the world (and so not a priori), or else conventions adopted for the purpose of constructing a satisfactory theoretical framework (and so not synthetic). And nearly everyone considered the causal laws of physics and chemistry to be both empirical and synthetic. There were, in fact, very few philosophers who accepted Kant's claim that synthetic a priori propositions exist. Most thought that:

1. If a proposition is a posteriori (i.e. a proposition whose truth is known by observation or experiment), then it is not necessary, and
2. If a proposition is necessary, then it is a priori (i.e. a proposition whose truth is knowable independent of the results of observations and experiments).

This was the starting point for nearly all philosophies of nature in the nineteenth and twentieth centuries, and it is still a widely accepted view.

Essentialists are not Kantians. Nor do they accept the standard position, which associates necessity exclusively with apriority, and contingency exclusively with what is a posteriori. Essentialists have a radically new category: the *necessary a posteriori*. Essentialists believe, for example, that the laws of nature are both necessary *and* a posteriori. They are a posteriori, because they have to be discovered by scientific investigation. But they are not analytically, or formally logically necessary, and they are not true by definition or convention. The laws of nature, they say, are *metaphysically* necessary, and therefore grounded in reality, and not in language. That water is H_2O, for example, is something that had to be discovered, and it is certainly not anything that could be known a priori. Nevertheless, it is a necessary proposition, because being H_2O is what it is to be water. It is not an analytic proposition that water is H_2O, because this is not what the word "water" means. Water would be H_2O, even if we had no word for water, or did not know what its chemical composition was. The fact that water is H_2O is therefore something that exists independently of language, and independently of our knowledge. Nevertheless, it is true that water is H_2O. Moreover, it is necessarily true, for there is no possible world in which what we call "water" would not be H_2O.

The proposition that water is H_2O is one of a very large number of propositions that are true in virtue of the essential properties of natural kinds, and all such propositions are not only true, but necessarily true. If the new essentialists are right, then all of the laws of nature are really like this. They are necessary in what is called the metaphysical, or *de re*, sense of necessity. They are true not in virtue of what things are *called*; they are true, rather, in virtue of what they *are*. Something might be called "water", even though it is not water. Or, something might be water, even though it is not called "water". So the truth of the proposition that water is H_2O is not determined by what water is called. According to the new essentialism, all true propositions attributing essential properties to natural kinds are necessarily true. Nevertheless, what the essential properties of the natural kinds are is an empirical question.

Essentialism is therefore a very radical doctrine. By rejecting the link between necessity and a priority, as it does, it flies in the face of both the Anglo-American and German traditions of metaphysics. If the new essentialists are right, then the laws of nature are both necessary and a posteriori.

Varieties of necessity

Essentialists have their own special brand of necessity. This kind of necessity has traditionally been called "metaphysical necessity", although the name is worrying to some, because it suggests, wrongly, that there is something speculative about it. The essentialists' brand of necessity might also be called "physical necessity", or "natural necessity", because it is the kind of necessity that essentialists believe to be characteristic of the laws of nature. But these terms do not indicate its special nature, and both are generally used to refer neutrally to that kind of necessity, whatever it might be, that is characteristic of the laws of nature. A better name would be its classical Latin name, "*de re* necessity", which might reasonably be translated as "real necessity", for this indicates the kind of grounding that essentialists believe natural necessities to have, namely, a grounding in reality. And this is the name we shall use mostly, although we shall also use the term "metaphysical necessity" on occasions. Real necessity is not, like "analyticity", grounded in the language that we use to describe the world, for really necessary connections would exist in nature, even if languages did not exist. Nor is it like "formal logical necessity", which is grounded in the laws of thought, for the laws of logic would be the same in any kind of world, but the really necessary connections that exist in nature are specific to worlds in which things of the same natural kinds as those existing in our world also exist. Nevertheless, real necessity is a species of strict necessity, for if a proposition is really necessary, then, like all the other kinds of strictly necessary propositions, it is true in every possible world.

By a possible world, I mean any world that might really exist. There are presumably many such possible worlds. Among the many worlds that might exist, there must be many that contain all of the kinds of things that actually exist in this world. These are of special interest, because all such worlds would belong to the same family as ours. In order for these worlds to exist, the things that exist in them must have the same natures as the things that exist here, for otherwise these things would not be things of the same kinds as those that exist in this world. Therefore, anything that is true of anything in virtue of its essential nature must be true of it in any other world in which it exists. Of course, there could also be worlds in which things of a kind that exist in this world do not exist at all. For example, there are presumably many possible worlds in which water does not exist. For every such world, the necessary proposition "Water is H_2O" would be vacuous. That is, there would be nothing in such a world for our word "water" to refer to. In formal logic, vacuous propositions are counted as true by default, and are described as "vacuously true". With this understanding, it is clear that "Water is H_2O" is a necessary proposition in the strict sense of being true in every possible world. In worlds where water exists, it is true by nature, and in worlds where water does not exist, it is vacuously true. Therefore, there cannot be a world in which water is not H_2O. The same is the case for all other really necessary propositions: they are all true in all possible worlds.

Real necessity is no less strict than any other kind of necessity. Many have speculated that natural necessity might be a much weaker kind of necessity, half-way between strict logical necessity and contingency. But, if essentialists are right, and the laws of nature are really necessary, then they must be counted as necessary in the very strong sense of being true in all possible worlds. Truth in all possible worlds is the defining characteristic of all forms of strict necessity. "A bachelor is an unmarried man", for example, is true in all possible worlds. Of course, there may well be worlds in which bachelors do not exist, or where there is no institution of marriage. In that case, the inhabitants of these worlds would not be described as bachelors, or as unmarried. Nevertheless, the sentence is a perfectly good sentence of English, and it would express the same truth in any world in which this language is spoken, even if none of its terms referred. If there are no bachelors, or men, or marriages in a given world, then the sentence will be non-referential. But it will still be a true sentence of the language. Formal logical truths are also true in all possible worlds, but for a different reason, for they will be true whatever the world is like. Formal logical truths have no subject matter, and are true solely in virtue of their logical form. But, just because they have no subject matter, if they are true in any world, then they must be true in every world. So, in general we can say that a proposition is strictly necessary, if and only if it is true in all possible worlds. In this sense, real necessities are just as strict as any others.

Real and imagined possibilities

There is an argument that Hume used over and over again, in both the *Treatise* and the *Enquiries*, to establish that causal connections are not strictly necessary. If any alleged causal connection were strictly necessary, he argued, then it would have to be logically impossible for the cause to occur, but the effect not to occur. However, the contrary of any causal law is always imaginable. Therefore, it is always logically possible for the cause to occur without the effect that it is supposed to produce. Therefore, he reasoned, if causal connections exist, they cannot be necessary connections. Hume was not, of course, making the obvious point that causal processes can always be interrupted, diverted or swamped by other processes. Everyone acknowledges that. Rather, he was arguing that, even without any defeaters or diverters, the effect need not occur, since the contrary is always imaginable.

So successful was Hume's strategy of argument that his conclusion that causal laws are not strictly necessary has been almost universally accepted. Until very recently, the generally accepted view of philosophers everywhere in the Anglo-American tradition was that causal laws are contingent, and have the status of empirical generalizations. Nevertheless, Hume's argument is unsound. For what is imaginable is not the same as what is really possible. While some states of affairs might be easily imaginable, it might, nevertheless, be impossible for them actually to occur.

One can easily imagine a bronze statue just dissolving into a heap of dust. If this were really to happen, it would be astonishing, but probably most philosophers would agree that it is logically possible. One can also imagine the same statue growing wings like a butterfly and fluttering away, or singing Christmas carols, or getting up and walking through a brick wall. Are these things all logically possible too? Probably most philosophers would concede that they are, since there are no evident contradictions involved in supposing that they happen. "Of course," they would say, "such things could not happen in the real world, because such happenings would be contrary to the laws of nature." But they are imaginable. And this, they would argue, is enough to show that they are logically possible.

However, imaginability is a very bad test of real possibility. It is true that there are no surface contradictions involved in the descriptions of these imagined happenings. But is this reason enough to think that such happenings are really possible? It would be, if anything could behave in any imaginable way, whatever its nature. But, if essentialists are right, and the identity of a thing depends on how it is constituted, it is not enough. If a thing's identity depends on what it is made of, or on how it is put together, then its identity must ultimately depend on the causal powers, capacities and propensities of its constituents. That is, the thing would not be what it is if its constituents did not have these causal powers. So a thing's behavioural possibilities must be restricted by its nature, and not determined by the powers of our imaginations.

The imaginability test of possibility derives from the assumption that what a thing can really do or become depends only on its manifest image, for this is what the imagination has to work with. It starts with the manifest image and transforms it. But why should we suppose that all imaginable transformations are possible? In supposing this, the imaginability test operates in the wrong way, and at the wrong level. It assumes bizarre phenomenological views of change, and of identity through change, for the test assumes that if the manifest image of something can be transformed by degrees into that of something else (as it nearly always can be), then this transformation is really possible for the things themselves. However, what it is really possible for a given thing to do or become does not depend only on the transformability of its manifest image. It depends also on what kind of thing it is, and how and of what it is constituted. A horse cannot, really cannot, be transformed into a cow, although an image of a horse can (easily with modern technology) be transformed into an image of a cow.

In considering questions of real possibility, it is important to keep the distinction between what a thing is, and what it looks like, clearly in mind. There might conceivably be a creature in some possible world that looks like a horse, which can indeed be transformed into something that looks like a cow. But it could not possibly *be* a horse, since horses are incapable of any such transformations. Nor could the result of the transformation *be* a cow, because cows cannot be produced in this way. It is like that stuff XYZ on "Twin Earth", which I mentioned earlier (p. 16). It may look like water, it may be called "water", and Twin Earth "people" may actually use it like water, but it cannot really *be* water if it is differently constituted, and so does not behave chemically as water does.

What a thing can do or become depends on the kind of thing it is. It does not depend on what it looks like, or what kind of thing we think it is. What we think is a horse might conceivably not be a horse. Therefore, it is epistemically possible that we are mistaken in thinking that something is a horse. Therefore, it is epistemically possible that the creature before us, which we take to be a horse, is not a horse. Therefore, it is epistemically possible that it could behave in ways that horses could not possibly behave. Therefore, if we can also be mistaken about the kind of world we inhabit (which of course we can), we must admit that it is epistemically possible that the thing in front of us could be transformed into something that looks like a cow.

113

But if the object in front of us is really a horse, then it cannot be so transformed, because it is not really possible for a horse to become a cow, or even to come to look like a cow. A horse could no more become a cow than it could become a banana. Nor could a horse even come to look like a banana, or any other kind of thing it does not already closely resemble.

The imaginability test of possibility thus confuses what is really or metaphysically possible with what is only epistemically possible. It purports to be a test of what could, really could, occur in some given circumstances, when in fact it tells us only what we are able consistently to imagine happening to things that are superficially like those that exist in these (or in superficially similar) circumstances.

The two concepts of possibility, epistemic and real, may indeed cut across one another. Not only might what is epistemically possible be really impossible, but the converse might also be true. What is epistemically impossible might really be possible, for what we are able to imagine is presumably conditioned, and hence limited, by our common experience of the middle-sized things we are familiar with. Consequently, what we may be able to imagine is unlikely to tell us much about what can really exist or occur at the truly macroscopic or microscopic level. If no process can be imagined by which a certain quantum effect can be produced, it does not follow that no such a process is possible.

There is, therefore, a vital distinction, on which every essentialist must insist, between what is epistemically possible and what is really or metaphysically possible. What is epistemically possible is just what is possible *for all we know*. It is therefore limited only by our knowledge, and perhaps also by our imaginations. But what is metaphysically possible depends on what is really the case. What it is possible for that thing to do is a function of its constitution and is limited by it. And this limitation exists whether or not we know what its constitution is.[19] Normally, the limits on behaviour imposed on

---

19. There is a serious problem here for essentialists, for real possibility would appear to be unknowable. There is no problem about knowing what is epistemically possible: possible for all we know. But how could we go on from there to find out what is really possible? Further research may reveal that what we thought was possible is really impossible (because it would require something to behave in a way that is contrary to its essential nature). But it would seem that no amount of research, short of a practical demonstration, can show that what is epistemically possible is also really possible. This is the essentialists' "problem of knowledge". We shall return to consider some of its implications in Chapter 7.

things by their constitutions are greater than those due to our knowledge, or to the powers of our imaginations. So, normally, what is epistemically possible will include what is metaphysically possible. But, just occasionally, reality may outstrip our imaginations, and there may be events or processes of kinds that we find unimaginable.

Defining the limits of the possible

Scientific essentialists hold that one of the primary aims of science is to define the limits of the possible. That is, it contends that scientists seek, wherever possible, to discover what can or cannot happen, depending on the circumstances, and, where something is found to be possible, to determine the probability of its happening. This thesis about the aim of science explains clearly the concern of physical natural scientists to discover the essential natures of things, and the laws of action of their dispositional properties. But books and articles on the philosophy of science seldom talk about this as a primary aim of scientific enquiry, and rarely mention it even as a secondary one. Normally, science is said to be engaged in a programme to discover what is true in general about the world. So science is seen as being concerned primarily with what is the case, rather than with what must be, or could be the case. Some philosophers have gone so far as to suggest that all talk of necessities or possibilities is "second-grade" discourse, which should ultimately be eliminated from science. A first-order extensional language, they say, that is, a language without such modalities as necessity and possibility operators, is all that should be needed.

If one is a Humean, such a focus on truth in an extensional language is natural enough, for, if the laws of nature are just universal generalizations about the world, as Humeans believe, then there is no place for the modalities of necessity or possibility to occur in their expression. Moreover, there cannot really be any modal properties in the world, that is, properties that describe what would or could happen in various kinds of circumstances. All such properties, it is said, must supervene on non-modal ones: a principle widely known as the "Humean supervenience thesis". According to this principle, if any modalities or modal properties occur in scientific discourse, they must, in principle, be eliminable. So the quest to define the limits of the possible is not seen by Humeans as being an important scientific goal. Why seek to discover what you must later seek to eliminate? The primary aim of science must be, rather, to describe reality as it is, and to reveal the regularities and patterns of behaviour that are to be found in it. It is not to discover what could, or would have to, happen in various kinds of mostly non-existent circumstances.

There are, however, insuperable difficulties with such a point of view. First, some laws of nature are explicitly modal (i.e. concerned with possibilities or necessities). The second law of thermodynamics, for example, is the principle of the *impossibility* of a perpetual motion machine of the second kind. It states that energy *cannot* systematically be transferred from a higher to a lower entropic state, for example, from a colder to a hotter body, without a net expenditure of energy in the process. This impossibility principle is manifestly not equivalent to the empirical generalization that there are no perpetual motion machines of the specified kind. It is not, for example, like the fact that there are no medieval steam engines. Pauli's exclusion principle is also explicitly modal. The fact that it reports is not just that no two electrons in an atom are ever in the same quantum state. Pauli's exclusion principle says that this is an impossibility: they *cannot be* in the same quantum state.

Secondly, the laws of nature that are not explicitly modal are all implicitly so, for no law of nature reports a mere accidental generalization. It is true that whenever water is electrolysed, hydrogen is released at the cathode and oxygen at the anode in the ratios by volume (under the same conditions of temperature and pressure) of two to one. But this is not only true, it is necessarily true. If the substance being electrolysed is water, it *must* yield hydrogen and oxygen in these proportions at these electrodes. If it did not do so, then it could not have been water in the first place. The same holds for all causal laws. It is not just that in these or those specific circumstances, such and such causes always do, as a matter of fact, have such and such effects. It is rather that they *must* have such effects in these circumstances.

The essentially modal character of causal laws is evidenced also by their restriction to ideal circumstances, for all causal laws contain riders excluding causal influences other than the ones that are being described. For example, when we say that an event of the kind A causes one of the kind B, we are not just saying that all As are Bs, *whatever* the circumstances, because, most probably, this is not true. Rather, what we are saying is that an event of the kind A would result in one of the kind B, if B were not somehow prevented from occurring. That is, the law says what would happen in these, presumably normal, circumstances. Causal laws therefore have the form of generalized conditionals. They say in general what would or might happen in various possible circumstances. They are not simple descriptions of what does happen in the actual circumstances. That being the case, an extensional language, which is fit only for describing what does happen, is not adequate for science. For science, we need a language with modalities (i.e. necessity and possibility operators) and causal conditionals (i.e. sentences that describe what would, or could, happen in various possible circumstances). Extensional languages are not rich enough for this task.

This point is now generally conceded, even by Humeans. They accept that science requires a modal language. Nevertheless, they continue to believe that a non-modal language (such as first-order predicate calculus) must be adequate for the complete description of the world, because, they say, there can be nothing more to the actual world than the things that actually exist, and the things they actually do. Specifically, they argue that there are no modal properties in nature. There are no potentialities, for example, or propensities, or dispositional properties of other kinds, which imply the existence of natural necessities in the world. All such properties, they say, must supervene somehow on the non-modal (categorical) properties of the things that actually exist, and so must ultimately be irrelevant to the description of the actual world.

If one accepts the Humean supervenience thesis, then the problem of explaining what natural necessities are, or what makes statements attributing modal properties to things true, becomes acute. Some Humeans have gone to quite extraordinary lengths to accommodate them, interpreting all statements attributing such properties to things as claims about relations holding between really existing possible worlds (Lewis 1986). But since every possible world, according to Humeanism, is a world without intrinsic modal properties, it is hard to see how this is supposed to solve the problem. A universe of worlds without intrinsic modal properties is a universe without causal powers.

Scientific essentialists reject the Humean conception of reality, and the supervenience thesis that it entails. They also reject the conception of the universe as an agglomeration of essentially non-modal possible worlds. From the perspective of the new essentialism, "possible worlds" semantics may be a useful model for the purposes for which it was constructed, but it is a model with no ontological significance. The actual world is a modal world, with in-built natural necessities.

And, if there are any other worlds that are at all like ours, then they too will be modal worlds.

The world as one of a kind

If natural necessities are grounded not in the actual world, but solely in relations between causally distinct (possible) worlds, none of which contain any causal powers or other modal properties, then natural necessities cannot necessitate. What does it matter how the actual world is related to other possible worlds if all the possible worlds are in themselves non-modal? If natural necessities exist, then they must be grounded in the actual world, and this world must itself have modal properties. Therefore, causal powers, capacities and propensities must exist in the actual world as essential properties of things, and be the source of its laws concerning these things. The more specific laws must, accordingly, be explications of the essential properties of the more specific kinds. The most general laws must be those describing the essential properties of the most general natural kinds, namely, those that are category-wide in scope. Such laws must apply to all things, or to all events and processes, or to all structures, depending on the categories over which they range.

There is, however, another, and probably equivalent, hypothesis about the grounding of the laws of nature, namely, that they all derive from the fact that the world itself is an instance of a natural kind. According to this global-kind hypothesis, the world is one that is distinguished from worlds of all other natural kinds by its global properties, and by its basic ontology. One reason for thinking that the world may be a member of a natural kind is that it has precisely the sorts of properties that one would expect of such a kind, for it is possible to say a great deal about the world as a whole. We can point to global structuring principles, universal processes of world evolution, general symmetries, a common ontological basis of reality, a single origin of the universe and various universally conserved quantities. Given a knowledge of these, we can say a great deal about what kinds of things can exist or occur in the world, or in any world that has the same structure and global properties as ours. The world we live in is not an amorphous or disconnected world, it seems, but a highly integrated and coherent structure.

First, we can say fairly confidently that ours is an expanding four-dimensional space-time world that is structured according to the principles of general relativity. Secondly, it is evident that the world has a global causal structure, for all of the events and processes occurring in the world (including the Big Bang and the process of inflation, if, indeed, there were such an event and such a process) consist ultimately of energy transmission processes, and the instantaneous changes of state by which such processes are initiated or terminated. Thirdly, the world is apparently one that displays certain global symmetries that are important for our understanding of what kinds of things and processes can occur. There is reason to believe that some of these symmetries may be broken from time to time. But, even if the symmetry principles are not strictly universal, they are expressible as conditional probabilities in which the *reference classes* are universal, that is, as principles attributing genuine dispositional properties to *all* events and processes, or to *all* physical systems: they are global *in scope*. Fourthly, the world is evidently a physical world, one that consists entirely of things that have energy, and that interact with each other physically, that is, energetically. A physical world is not the only conceivable kind of world. Indeed, if dualist interactionism were true, then the world would not be a purely physical world. Fifthly, the world appears to be universally conservative with respect to a number of quantities, including energy, momentum, angular momentum, charge and several others. Consequently, the world would seem to be one in which only certain kinds of changes are possible, namely, those that are not forbidden by the conservation laws. Again, a caveat may be necessary. If some symmetries can sometimes be broken, then maybe some of these quantities are not always strictly conserved. However, even if this is the case, the world's high degree of conservativeness with respect to these quantities is still a global fact about reality, and so, plausibly, characteristic of the kind of world in which we live. Finally, the world is evidently one that is made up of a relatively small number of interrelated kinds of fundamental particles and fields, and it is plausible to suppose that when we know more about the basic structure of the world we shall be able to explain why these, and perhaps only these, particular kinds of particles and fields can exist. Certainly, if John Barrow, Frank Tipler, John Leslie and other writers on cosmology are right, then the global properties of worlds of the kind in which we live are at least highly restrictive of the kinds of things that can exist in worlds like ours. It might even be the case that no things, other than things of the kinds that do exist in our world, could exist in any world with the same global properties.

Currently accepted theory may not, of course, be right in detail. But no one doubts that there are global properties and structure. And the fact that these global properties and this structure exist at all implies that the world is a unified whole. If the world consisted of unrelated kinds of things that were just thrown together somehow, these properties and this structure would be inexplicable. On the other hand, the existence of these properties and structure is sufficient to explain a great deal of what happens in the world. Certainly, they greatly restrict the range of possible kinds of things and occurrences.

Therefore, we seem to be able to characterize the world, and explain why it behaves as it does, in much the same kind of way as we might characterize an electromagnetic field or a water molecule, and explain why it does the things it does. Electromagnetic fields and water molecules are clearly instances of natural kinds. It is plausible, therefore, to suppose that the world itself is an instance of a natural kind. If one does not accept a theological theory of laws, it is hard to see how else, or how better, to explain the existence of all this global structure.

If the world in which we live is a member of a natural kind, then its essential properties and structures will be those that any member of this kind must have, by virtue of its being a member of this kind, and that no member of the kind could lack. Thus no member of the specific kind to which our world belongs could possibly lack any of the *fundamental* properties that exist in our world. Nor could it fail to have the spatiotemporal–structural possibilities that must exist if the structures that exist in fundamental objects or processes are to be possible, for the possibility of their existence is a necessary condition for the possibility of existence of the things that constitute our world. Therefore, any world of the same natural kind as ours must contain the same fundamental properties, and have the same spatiotemporal–structural possibilities, as ours.

The hypothesis that the world is a member of a natural kind thus leads to the conclusion that the actual world is one in which things have their fundamental properties necessarily. It thus enables us to explain what natural necessity is for our world, and, incidentally, for any other worlds of the same natural kind as ours. What is *naturally necessary* in our world is what must be true in any world of the same natural kind. What is *naturally possible* is what might be true in a world of the same natural kind as ours. What is *naturally contingent* is what might or might not be true in a world that is essentially the same as ours.

120

Is metaphysical necessity too strong?

While many philosophers may be sympathetic to the idea that the laws of nature are in some sense necessary, and immanent in the world, they are likely to balk at the claim that they are metaphysically necessary. This seems far too strong, for it implies that the laws are true in all possible worlds, just as formal logical and analytic propositions are. But how can an essentialist possibly be in a position to assert such a thing? They must say, for example, that it is metaphysically necessary that every causal process is intrinsically conservative of energy, and other universally conserved quantities. Why? Because, they say, it would not be a causal process of the global kind to which all events and processes occurring in this world belong if it were not conservative of these quantities. If a process were not conservative of these quantities, they must say, then it would not be a process of a kind that could occur in our world, or in any other world of the same natural kind as ours. Bold claims indeed! But what evidence could an essentialist possibly have for them? How do we know what kind of world we live in, or what kinds of objects, events or structures are possible in our kind of world?

The fact is that we don't know, and essentialists do not pretend to know. However, the conservation laws are well established, and what one can reasonably say is that if they are true, then they are necessarily true. They are necessarily true, if they are true at all, because what is true of the most general kinds of objects and events in this world must be true of the most general kinds of objects and events in all worlds of the same natural kind as ours. Such is the nature of natural kind reasoning.

Of course, the world might not be the kind of world we think it is. But this speculation trades on uncertainty, and is therefore of an epistemic nature. Of course, it is *epistemically* possible that the world is a very different kind of world from the kind we think it is. There might well be, for all we know, all sorts of monsters lurking in the dark, or in the future yet to be discovered, which violate these laws, in which case we may have to conclude that the world is truly, and perhaps necessarily, very different from the way we think it is. But epistemic possibility is not real possibility, and ignorance is not a source of knowledge. If you want to know what kind of world we actually live in, and therefore what is true of all worlds of the same natural kind as ours, you have to rely on the best theories available to you, and, according to these theories, all events and processes are intrinsically conservative of a number of well-known quantities.

There is no serious objection, therefore, to accepting the strong view that the laws of nature are *all* metaphysically necessary. The more specific laws of nature, the causal and structural laws, which depend on the causal powers and structures of the more specific kinds of things existing in the world, are undoubtedly metaphysically necessary. Essentialists argue that the most general laws of nature are laws of the same kind, but, because we are world-bound, we cannot stand outside of the worlds to designate the natural kind of world to which our own world belongs. We can only designate it internally, postulate that it is one of a kind (for the sorts of reasons that have been elaborated), point to the kinds of objects, events and structures which actually exist in our world, and try to say what their essential natures are. If we are right about all of these things, then what we assert to be true about the most general kinds of things existing in this world will be necessarily true.

CHAPTER 7

Philosophical Implications

The nature of metaphysics

The new essentialism is a metaphysic that has implications for philosophy right across the board, in ontology, epistemology, logic, theology, social theory, philosophy of science and most other areas. It is a thesis about the sources of power in the world, about the nature of reality, about the connections between things, about logical analysis, and even about the methodology of philosophical enquiry. As the dominant metaphysic, the Humeanism with which I have sought to contrast essentialism also has broad implications in philosophy. It is also not just a theory of science, or language, or of what exists, but a metaphysic that gives shape to contemporary theories in all of these areas.

A metaphysic cannot be judged as a more specific philosophical theory might be. It is so wide-ranging that it has to be argued for in a different way. One cannot say "Here are the problems; here is the solution", and then argue that this solution is better than any other, for the problems shift from one metaphysical position to another. Thus, for a Humean, there are two serious problems about the laws of nature: the necessity problem (to explain the nature, or the illusion, of physical necessity) and the idealization problem (to explain the existence of laws that appear to range over idealized systems, e.g. closed and isolated ones). For an essentialist, these are not serious problems. Physical necessity is just metaphysical necessity, and the focus of theory on idealized systems is due to the focus of science on the intrinsic natures of things. On the other hand, there is a problem of knowledge for essentialists. No doubt many things that are epistemically possible are really impossible, and perhaps, occasionally, there are things that are epistemically impossible that are really possible. Epistemic possibility is easily determined: a supposition is epistemically possible, if there is no obvious contradiction involved in making it. But how can we ever find out which of the epistemic possibilities are real possibilities?

Because of its basic role in shaping philosophical theories, a metaphysic has to be argued for, and defended, on many different fronts at the same time. And there is really only way of doing this, namely, to write a book setting out the position carefully, displaying its range and overall coherence, contrasting it with other positions, showing how it deals with philosophical issues in various fields, and answering specific objections. If your system strikes your readers as being simpler, more coherent, or more promising as a way of thinking about the world, better able to deal with the recalcitrant difficulties of other systems, and does not throw up too many problems of its own, then these may be good enough reasons to adopt it. To try to argue for a new metaphysic point by point is difficult, because a metaphysic determines a whole mind-set, and to adopt a new metaphysic is, necessarily, to undergo a revolution in one's thinking about things.

Historians of science are familiar with the processes that form the background to scientific revolutions, for all such revolutions occur against some pre-existing orthodoxy. In science, orthodoxy consists of doing standard work within some widely accepted tradition. Thomas Kuhn calls this background orthodoxy the practice of "normal science". Normal science, he says, is the articulation and development of scientific paradigms. Precisely what a paradigm is, or how it is embodied, is sometimes hard to say, but a paradigm is probably best thought of as a broadly based and well-established research tradition. Such a tradition can be said to exist in a given area, if there is basic agreement among the professionals working in the area (a) on the general principles involved, (b) about what the major problems of the area are, (c) about how one should go about trying to solve these problems, and (d) on what would constitute an acceptable solution. Major paradigms in the history of science include Ptolemaic astronomy, Newtonian physics, Avogadro's atomic–molecular theory, Darwinian natural selection and Freudian psychology, but there are a great many lesser paradigms than these. Often such a research tradition was originally founded on a single major work (whence the name "paradigm"), whose influence persisted long after it was published.

But sometimes a paradigm can evolve with a growing consensus about the basic issues involved. The relativistic Hot Big Bang theory of the origin of the universe is, perhaps, a case in point.

Kuhn argues that normal science is a vital part of the process of theoretical development, even if, on its own terms, it ends in failure. For it is the failures of normal science that generate the theoretical anomalies that lead eventually to revolutionary developments. Science can put up with some anomalies, Kuhn says, and may do so for many years, in the hope that a solution compatible with the assumptions of normal science will eventually be found. But anomalies can eventually become overwhelming, and scientists working in a given field may begin to have serious doubts about the theoretical stance they have taken. The science is then in a state of crisis. When a science enters into a period of crisis, Kuhn says, a new phase of theoretical development occurs. Professionals working in the field begin overtly to question some of the fundamental assumptions they have been making, and exploring other ways of handling the data. The scientific debate becomes much more questioning, reflective and philosophical.

Philosophy, too, has its paradigms. The major ones include the Platonic and Aristotelian ones of ancient times, the natural theological paradigm of St Thomas Aquinas, the rationalist metaphysics of Descartes, the mechanistic paradigm of Locke and Boyle, the Leibnizian, Humean, Kantian, Hegelian and Marxian metaphysical systems of the eighteenth and nineteenth centuries, the Fregean paradigm in logic, and logical positivism, Heideggerianism and analytic philosophy in the twentieth century. Of these, some are subordinate to others, as Marxism is to Hegelianism, and logical positivism is to Humeanism. That is, there is a clear ancestral relationship holding between them. Moreover, some of these paradigms continue to hold sway in the fields in which they initially gained prominence, as Humeanism does in the realms of causation and laws of nature. Some also continue to exert a major influence through their philosophical offspring, as Humeanism does through the Kantian, positivist and analytic philosophical traditions it spawned.

The new essentialism is a development of the older Aristotelian paradigm, and so runs counter to most of the modern trends in philosophy. To borrow a phrase from Herbert Butterfield, it requires a different kind of thinking cap. It is not an offshoot of any of the main traditions of philosophy that have emerged since the scientific revolution of the seventeenth century, for these traditions were all developed in reaction to Aristotelianism, and were consciously supportive

125

of a Newtonian world-view, rather than an Aristotelian one. The new essentialism is accordingly very different from the other philosophical traditions that have been developed in modern times. Its acceptance requires a different programme of analysis in philosophy – one that might aptly be called "realistic analysis" (in order to distinguish it from the kinds of semantic and "possible worlds" analyses standardly employed in philosophy) – a different view of the aim and structure of physical theory, different conceptions of causation and laws of nature, different views about necessities and possibilities and, ultimately, a different theory about the nature of logic. The new essentialism also has implications for the social sciences, and the kinds of theories that one can expect to develop in these areas.

Most of these changes are required in order to accommodate the idea that the world consists not of essentially passive things, but of intrinsically active ones. One cannot, for example, think of a property as just a set of objects in some domain or other (as logicians in the Fregean tradition do), as though the property has no powers, but is just a way of classifying the objects in this domain. If the causal powers of things are real properties, then things must be disposed to behave in certain ways in virtue of having these properties. The bearers of these properties must therefore stand in the relation of potential primary participant in a certain natural kind of process: a causal process. Such facts as these must somehow gain recognition in our formal semantics and logical analyses.

Logical analysis

Essentialism has implications for modal semantics, and for the philosophical programme known as logical analysis. It cuts away their metaphysical foundations, and leaves them stranded.

The belief that nature is intrinsically powerless, and that the laws of nature are brute general facts about how the intrinsically powerless things in the world are or behave, leads naturally enough to certain ways of representing the world in our theorizing. For example, it encourages us to think of the world as a totality of self-contained logically independent facts, or states of affairs, more or less as Russell did, since what exists at any one place or time, we are led to believe, must be independent of what exists at any other place or time. Given this conception of reality, it is hard to think of the laws of nature as anything other than universal regularities that happen to exist within

126

this totality of facts. However, this belief about nature and its laws cannot be sustained in an essentialist world-view.

In general, our descriptions of the world will be true, if they correspond to the facts. Given a Humean conception of reality, these facts must all be non-modal. That is, they can neither be, nor imply, any statements of necessity or possibility. Therefore, according to Humeanism, the true descriptions of the world can make no reference to the causal powers of things, unless these properties can be reduced, somehow, to non-modal ones. The primary problem for the theory of truth, therefore, is seen as being to develop a non-modal (i.e. extensional) language that is adequate for describing the world, and a correspondence theory of truth that is adequate to explain what makes any true statement expressible in this language true.

The theory of truth-preservation, and therefore the theory required as the foundation for modern logic, must likewise depend on the development of such languages and appropriate theories of truth for them. A Humean conception of reality thus lies behind, and motivates, the development of extensional logics with extensional semantics, and underwrites the deployment of such languages for describing the world. Given this conception of reality, the laws of nature are, naturally enough, supposed to relate classes of things, rather than describe their causal powers. The law that all As are Bs, for example, becomes simply the fact that the class of As is included in the class of Bs. There is no suggestion that there might be, let alone must be, a reason why As are Bs, if in fact it is a law that all As are Bs. Nor is there any suggestion that the required reason must have something to do with what it is for something to be an A. Indeed, the idea that there might be some connection between a thing's being an A and its being a B, which is responsible for its being a law that all As are Bs, just drops out of the picture.

In many cases, truth seems to be simply a relationship of correspondence with non-modal facts. If something is referred to by name, and something is then said about it, then what is said is true if and only if what is referred to is the way it is said to be. This seems obvious. However, there are many different kinds of propositions that are held to be true or false, including many whose relationship to reality is quite obscure. The programme of trying to specify realistic truth conditions for these more troublesome propositions, including statements of laws and causal connections, was a preoccupation of philosophers for most of the twentieth century. One way of dealing with them was that pioneered by Russell, Moore and others. These philosophers sought to analyse the troublesome propositions logically, so that their truth or falsity could be derived from that of more elementary propositions whose truth or falsity conditions were not thought to be problematic, or, at any rate, were thought to be less problematic than those that were to be analysed. This was the programme known as "logical analysis".

This programme of analysis has often been pursued subject to two important constraints. The first of these is the *requirement of extensionality*, which is dictated by Humeanism, and is a constraint on the kind of analysis that is acceptable. To explain what makes a given proposition true, it is supposed that we must be able to express this proposition in an extensional language, that is, a language whose terms refer to things in a specific domain, and whose predicates refer to sets of things in this domain. It is not a language in which we can refer to the *natural kinds* or *natural properties* of things that exist in this domain, or say which of these properties are their essential properties. Languages like natural languages, in which reference can be made to such properties and kinds, are therefore not extensional languages.

The second common constraint on the adequacy of any proposed analysis is the *requirement of realism*. The domain in which the language is interpreted must be a domain of real things. One cannot accept as satisfactory an analysis that refers to a domain of things one does not believe in, for the aim of the programme is to explain the manner in which true propositions correspond to reality. It is to specify the truth-makers for the propositions we believe to be true, and explain the nature of the relationship of correspondence between the truth-makers and the propositions they make true. It is not good enough, for example, to say that "$2 + 2 = 4$" is true if and only if "$x + x = y$" is satisfied by the sequence $<2, 2, 4>$ if one does not believe in numbers. The programme aims to provide *realistically* acceptable truth conditions, in which reference is made to real existents. If any otherwise satisfactory analysis failed to meet this requirement, then an analysis of the analysandum (i.e. the analysis that has been given) would be needed.

The programme of analysis has often been pursued without much regard for the requirement of realism. "Possible worlds" analyses of modal and conditional propositions would seem to violate this requirement. Of course, there are some philosophers who think that these analyses do satisfy the requirement of realism. They believe in possible worlds. But there are many more who do not think this, and who, accordingly, have sought to analyse propositions about possible worlds so that they can be realistically understood. There are also some purists who consider the question of the reality of possible worlds to be relatively unimportant. What interests them is what can be done with this kind of analysis by ringing the changes on the formal relationships that may be supposed to hold between possible worlds.

The main trouble with "possible worlds" realism is that the only reason anyone has, or ever could have, to believe in other possible worlds (other than this one) is that they are needed, apparently, to provide truth conditions for modals and conditionals. They are needed, it seems, because if this world were the only reality, and reality is non-modal, then there would not be enough reality to go around. The truths expressed in modal and conditional propositions are left with nothing in the Humean non-modal actual world to correspond to. To explain what makes them true, it seems, we should need things that could or might exist, as well as the things that do exist. Therefore, it is argued, this world cannot be all there is. There must be other possible worlds too: worlds that are not actual, but merely possible.

This is why some philosophers who are not prone to believing in fairy tales really do believe in the existence of merely possible worlds. It is, indeed, the only legitimate reason anyone could possibly have for believing in the existence of any such world. There could not be a good reason of another kind for believing in such a world, because, if there were such a reason, the world in question would not be merely possible. Suppose, for example, that, according to some accepted symmetry principle, there must exist a kind of mirror image of this world from which we have been causally isolated since the Big Bang. If we really believed in this symmetry principle, then of course we should not regard this other world as being merely possible. We should simply think of it as a remote and inaccessible branch of our own world.

The argument that belief in the existence of merely possible worlds cannot be independently justified looks like a devastating argument against any literal interpretation of possible worlds theory. Moreover, if the correspondence theory of truth requires such an interpretation, then this is a devastating argument against the correspondence theory. If you have to invent an infinity of possible worlds, for which you could not possibly have any other evidence, just to save your theory, then your theory cannot be much good. This would be ad-hocism with a vengeance (see Ellis 1990: part II).

But maybe one does not have to be a realist about possible worlds to save the correspondence theory of truth. The failure of the programme of analysis to discover realistic truth conditions may be due to something else. It may be due to the inherent Humeanism of the programme. Indeed, the programme is not only Humean, but it is also nominalistic, and does not even recognize the existence of genuine properties and relations, for one does not have properties or relations in this tradition; one only has predicates. One does not have names denoting kinds of things, like copper or tigers; one has the predicates "is copper" or "is a tiger". Properties, relations and kinds of substances, if they can be talked about at all, are identified with their extensions. The property of being yellow is the set of all yellow things. The relation of being greater in mass than is the set of ordered pairs x and y such that x is greater in mass than y. The substance, copper, is the set of all things that are coppery. It is as if the world consisted just of individuals and sets of individuals, as indeed Quine, Smart and many other Humeans once believed.

However, the world certainly consists of things belonging to other ontological categories, and to describe it adequately we need a language in which we can talk about and relate these different kinds of things. The failure of the programme of analysis may therefore be due simply to the poverty of the semantic theory on which it depends, and ultimately to the poverty of Humeanism. If the ontology of the real world is as rich as essentialists believe it to be, the problem of specifying realistic truth conditions for modals and conditionals is unlikely to be overcome, unless we start with a much richer base than the lean ontology of things and sets of things accepted by many logical analysists. To deal with this problem, we should begin to construct our programme of analysis on the basis of an ontology that also includes natural kinds of objects and processes, and dispositional properties of various kinds, so that natural modalities may be explained with reference to things existing in the actual world. The programme should not be one that seeks to reduce everything at the outset to individual things and sets of things. The implications of essentialism for modal semantics and for the philosophical programme of logical analysis are therefore likely to be very great indeed.

Necessities and possibilities

According to "possible worlds" realists, the actual world is just one of infinitely many possible worlds: the one we happen to inhabit. Otherwise, there is nothing special about it. A possible world is real, "possible worlds" realists say, if it is consistently describable. But it is not the actual world, unless the world described is the one in which we live. The word "actual" in the phrase "actual world" is thus to be understood as one that serves to locate ourselves in the realm of possibilities.

For an essentialist, however, this usage is problematic. It is problematic because essentialists are *modal realists*. They wish to make a distinction that is directly applicable to the actual world between what is really possible, and what is not – a distinction that does not commit them to the existence of any worlds other than the actual world. What is really possible, they say, is what is compatible with the natures of things in this world. So, if it is really possible that something-or-other will occur, then it is possible that there is a world of the same natural kind as ours in which it does occur. Real possibility is thus to be seen as depending on the real properties of things existing in the actual world, rather than on relationships between the actual world and other merely possible worlds.

Correspondingly, essentialists argue that what is really necessary is what must hold in any world of the same natural kind as ours, that is, any world with the same basic ontology as ours. Thus, according to essentialists, both real necessities and real possibilities are grounded in the actual world, rather than in relationships between this world and other possible worlds. If other worlds exist, essentialists say, then they are not merely possible, but actual. They just happen to be located in other spatiotemporal or causal frameworks, if, indeed, they are sufficiently like our world to have such frameworks. But neither their existence nor their properties are in any way relevant to what is really possible or really necessary in the actual world.

Real necessities and possibilities may easily be relativized. Thus, we may talk about what is "now really possible", meaning what is really possible from now on, given our history to date, or what was really possible yesterday, meaning what is really possible, given our history up to yesterday. In a deterministic world, these distinctions would be pointless. But in an indeterministic world such as ours, there are clear differences between what is really possible (timelessly), what is now possible and what was possible yesterday.

Real necessities and possibilities may also be conditionalized in various ways. For example, we may speak of what is really necessary, that is, what would really have to be the case, *if* certain conditions are, or had been, or were to be, fulfilled. Or, we may speak of what is really possible, that is, what really might be the case, *if* certain conditions are, or had been, or were to be, fulfilled. Thus, we may easily develop a modal semantics for conditionals, based on the essentialist thesis that there are real necessities and possibilities in nature. There is no need for the elaborate paraphernalia of "possible worlds", "counterparts" in other possible worlds, or "similarity relationships" between worlds, that are required for "possible worlds" semantics. Thus, the new essentialism promises an enormous simplification of the semantics required for modal and conditional logics.

There is, however, a serious problem with such realistic semantics for modal and conditional logics. It is the one we signalled earlier as the problem of knowledge of real possibilities. It arises in this way: to evaluate a conditional on this semantics (i.e. decide whether or not it is true), we should have to consider what would happen, or be likely to happen, in a world of the same natural kind as ours in which the antecedent condition is satisfied, other things being as near as possible to the way they actually are. The proposition "if A were the case, then B would be the case" will be true on the new theory if and only if in any world of the same natural kind as ours in which A is true, in circumstances as near as possible to those that actually obtain, B must also be true. The difficulty is that far too many conditionals are likely, on careful analysis, to have impossible antecedents, and therefore turn out to be just vacuously true, for, although it may be easy enough for us to *imagine* a world very like ours in which a false antecedent is true, it may well be really impossible that there should be such a world.

The resolution of this difficulty has important implications for both the methodology of philosophical enquiry and the nature of logic. First, essentialists cannot conduct philosophical investigations in the same debonair fashion as Humeans, allowing their imaginations free rein in the construction of metaphysically possible worlds. They have to be much more aware of the limitations of the imagination as an instrument for determining what is, or is not, really possible. The requirement of realism thus makes heavy demands on any theory that seeks to specify truth conditions for conditionals. As philosophers, we have been systematically trained to think that whatever is imaginable is possible. This is part of our Humean upbringing. Because we have been trained in this way, it is very easy for us to confuse epistemic possibility with real possibility. If it is imaginable, we are apt to suppose, then it must be at least logically possible.

Take almost any philosophical paper written in the Anglo-American tradition. In it you will find examples of allegedly possible states of affairs. These supposedly possible states of affairs, which are

drawn from the imagination, are the examples and counter-exar
used by philosophers in our tradition in their arguments fo
philosophical positions they are defending. But our imagina
work without scientific constraint, and hence without havin
consider the sorts of limitations on possibilities that exist in the
world. Consequently, the examples used by philosophers often s
absurd to scientists, and to others who are not well trained
philosophy, and it has to be explained patiently that, as philosoph
we are concerned not with *physical* possibility, but only with *log*
possibility, the test for which, apart from there being no obvic
contradiction in describing the case, is just imaginability or conce
ability. At any rate, what is possible is supposed to have nothing to
with what is possible from a scientific point of view.

The methodology of testing philosophical positions by usir
imaginatively constructed but scientifically implausible, or eve
physically impossible, counter-examples is a reasonable one if you ar
a Humean, and believe that all events are loose and separate. In
Humean world, anything that is consistently imaginable is possible
because the laws of nature in such a world can always be changed to
make it conform to the way we imagine it to be. The identities and
natures of things never get in the way. But in the kind of world that
science has revealed to us, we can no longer be so sanguine about the
looseness or separateness of things; and our imaginations, which are
necessarily superficial and cartoon-like in their representations, can
no longer be considered reliable sources of information about real
possibilities. An essentialist must, therefore, be much more cautious
than a Humean when making judgements about what is really
possible.

According to the essentialist semantics that has been outlined, a
counter-factual conditional will be only vacuously true if its antecedent condition is really impossible. But, at this point, the problem
of knowledge of real possibilities (Bigelow 1999) raises its ugly head
It is easy enough to decide whether the antecedent of a condition
describes an epistemic possibility. If there is no obvious reason why
is impossible, this is enough to justify the claim that it is epistemica
possible. But it is not enough to show that it is really possible. The
fore, if the significance of a conditional depends on the real possibi
of its antecedent, there is a serious problem of knowledge concern
conditionals. How can we know whether a given counter-fac
conditional is significant, that is, not just vacuously true? There
some counter-factual conditionals with antecedents that are obvic

133

physically impossible, such as "If we could walk on water, then we should have less need for boats." It would not matter at all if these turned out to be vacuously true. It would be a serious problem for a modal semantics, however, if many quite ordinary-looking counter-factuals, such as "If I had a cold beer in front of me, then I should drink it", were to turn out to be vacuous.

The best way of dealing with this difficulty is to concede that many counter-factuals, and perhaps also some ordinary indicative condi-tionals, might turn out to be vacuous, but to argue that what matters for conditionals is not whether they are non-vacuously true, but whether they are *assertable*. If the antecedent of a conditional cannot, for some reason, be fulfilled, the conditional may nevertheless be assertable, for it may well provide accurate and relevant information about the dispositional properties of its subject matter in spite of this. Consider the proposition "If there were a beer in front of me, then I should drink it." It is a fact about me that I am thirsty. It is also a fact that I like beer, and that there is nothing in the world that I would like better at the moment. Consequently, it is entirely appropriate for me to say "If there were a beer in front of me, then I should drink it." It simply does not matter whether it is really possible for there to be a beer in front of me. By asserting the conditional I tell you graphically what my desires are at the present time, and what you could do to satisfy them. It is better than saying "I am thirsty", because you might then offer me a glass of water, which is not what I want. It is also better than saying "I am thirsty, and I like beer", because this is compatible with my not wanting a beer at the moment. The sentence "If there were a beer in front of me, then I should drink it" expresses my desires clearly and precisely, even though they will not, and perhaps cannot, be immediately satisfied. In this case, and in the case of many other conditionals, the implications of assertability turn out to be much more important than those of the truth of what is being asserted.

The problem of induction

Essentialism has profound implications for the theory of rationality. In particular, it promises to transform our thinking about scientific rationality and the theory of inductive reasoning. If one believes, as Hume did, that all events are loose and separate, then the problem of induction is probably insoluble. Anything could happen. But if one

thinks, as essentialists do, that the laws of nature are immanent in the world, and depend on the essential natures of things, then there are strong constraints on what could possibly happen. If the new essentialists are right, then things must act in ways that depend on their intrinsic properties or structures, and on how these things stand in relationship to other things. Consequently, it is a necessary truth that things of the same natural kind must always behave in exactly the same ways (or range of ways with the same probabilities), if they are in circumstances of the same kind.

From a Humean point of view, the problem of induction is concerned with justifying inferences from what is known to have occurred on some occasions to what will occur (or has occurred) on other occasions. There can be no doubt that the probability of a random sample matching the total population from which it was drawn increases with the size of the sample. This is true however large the population may be, and this fact is mathematically demonstrable. But there remains a philosophically disturbing problem concerning our knowledge that a given sample is random with respect to the properties in which we are interested. Observations of European swans never really justified the inference of the conclusion that all swans are white, because, with respect to this property (namely, whiteness), the sample was not random: the observations were too local. However, all of our observations are local in this sense. They are made by us, in our own time and in our own region of the universe. So the question arises, how can we possibly infer from observations made locally anything about what is true universally? Might we not all be in the position of Australian aborigines, who falsely believed that all swans are black?

From the point of view of an essentialist, the problem of induction appears very different, for it reduces to that of discovering what natural kinds there are, and identifying their essential properties and structures. Essentialists hold that once we know the essential natures of things, we know how they must be disposed to behave whenever or wherever, or in whatever world, they might exist. There is no problem of inference from some to all, therefore. The presumption is, rather, in favour of strict uniformity. If there is good reason to believe that something is a member of a natural kind, and good reason to think that it has such and such a nature, then there is good reason to think that everything of that kind must have this same nature.

There are, of course, problems lurking here too. How are the natural kinds to be identified, and how are their essential natures to be discovered? But they are different problems from the Humean ones, and do not lead to sceptical doubts about our knowledge of the future, or of the distant past. There can be legitimate doubts about whether two things are members of the same natural kind, or whether the properties or structures that have been postulated as essential really are essential. For example, it may be doubted whether a proposed biological mechanism does what it is supposed to do. But these are the kinds of doubts and concerns that working scientists are accustomed to, and know how to handle. They are not irresolvable sceptical doubts like those generated by Humeanism.

The essentialist's world is a bound and connected world of the kind that science generally presupposes. If what we take to be the same natural kind of thing recurs, and we do something of the same sort to it, then we should expect it to respond as any member of that kind must respond, *qua* member of that kind. Specifically, it should display the essential dispositional properties of things of that kind for which the action we took is a trigger. If it does do so, then there is nothing to explain, except how the process works. If it does not do so, then the question arises, why should this thing be different from other things of its kind? There are many possibilities: (a) the thing does not belong to the natural kind to which it appears to belong (it might, for example, be a different species of the same generic kind), or (b) what we did to it was not an effective trigger (i.e. did not belong to the appropriate natural kind of activating events), or (c) we were mistaken about what the essential properties of the kind are, or (d) the expected effect did occur, but was masked by other events and so on.

So, for an essentialist, the problem of induction has a rather different flavour. It is not a question of justifying the inference from "all observed As are Bs" to "all As are Bs". This inference would be justified automatically if we had good reason to believe that the As we had observed belonged to a natural kind, and that the property of being a B was due to the essential nature of As. In that case, the problem would be, rather, to explain the failure of such an inference. Where we have a case of inductive failure, there are many possible explanations that must be sorted through, and the scientific task is to do this, eliminate alternatives and determine which of the remaining alternatives provides the best explanation. We might decide that the class designated by A is not a natural kind class, or that there are no essential properties of As in virtue of which they are Bs, so that if an A is a B, then this is just an accident, or that the apparent exceptions are either not really As, or they really are Bs (i.e. monster-barring and monster-adjustment), or any of a number of other things. But whatever we decide, we will have learned something from our experience, and our conceptualization of the world will have been improved.

If the laws of nature are not imposed upon the world, but arise from the essential natures of things in the world, then it is metaphysically impossible for things to behave in any of the bizarre ways envisaged by some philosophers. Emeralds cannot all turn blue in the year 2050, for example (as Nelson Goodman (1955) envisaged), because to do so they would have to have an extrinsically variable nature. But the essential nature of a thing cannot be dependent on anything that is extrinsic, such as the date or place of its existence, or whether or not, or how often, it has been observed. Consequently, date-dependent properties, such as those postulated by Nelson Goodman in his various examples, cannot be essential properties. Therefore, it makes a great deal of difference whether one thinks of the laws of nature as impositions on a passive world, or as arising out of its nature. If they are imposed on a passive world, then anything goes. But if they derive from the essential properties of things, then they cannot be dependent on the specific circumstances of their existence.

The programme of realistic analysis

If the new essentialism is accepted, philosophy must change direction. In metaphysics, it must focus on reality, rather than on language or the visual image, for all of the important concepts of essentialist metaphysics are grounded in reality, not in how we may talk about or imagine reality to be. The important modalities for metaphysics are real possibilities and necessities, because their epistemic counterparts are grounded in ignorance rather than knowledge. If something is epistemically possible, then this is only because we have no sufficient warrant for believing that it is really impossible. If it is epistemically necessary, then it is just because we cannot conceive it to be false. If something is epistemically probable, then this is because our reasons for believing it seem stronger than those for disbelieving it. But if reality is our focus, then none of these epistemic concepts is of primary importance. What matters is how the world is; and this is ultimately for our science to tell us.

The epistemic concepts become the main concern only when we step away from reality to think about our thinking about it. They are of primary importance for the theory of rationality, for example, where what is at issue are questions about the coherence and explanatory adequacy of our belief systems. Logic, as I have argued elsewhere (Ellis 1979), should be regarded as the theory of rational belief systems, rather than the theory of truth, or truth preservation.

The new essentialism must also lead to a turning away from semantic analysis as a fundamental tool for the pursuit of metaphysical aims, for semantics is concerned with the relationships between words and the world, and so how we think about and represent the world in language. But there is no reason to think that the language we speak accurately reflects the kind of world we live in. From the fact that something is not evidently self-contradictory, for example, we are likely to conclude that it is really possible. Nevertheless, this may not be so. Our everyday language just reflects our naive judgements of what could, or could not, occur in the world, not judgements based on a scientific understanding of things.

Analytic and formal logical truths are necessarily true. I have no quarrel with this. But not all necessary truths are either analytic or formal logical. Most metaphysically necessary truths, for example, are synthetic, since they are not true in virtue of the meanings of words. The grounds of their truth lie in the natures of the kinds of things to which reference is made. Consequently, there must be many truths which are at once synthetic, necessary and a posteriori. The proposition that helium has atomic number 2, for example, is not analytic, since its truth does not depend on the meanings of words; it is necessary, since nothing could have atomic number 2 without being a species of helium, and it is a posteriori, since it had to be established empirically that the element responsible for the mysterious Fraunhofer lines in the solar spectrum has atomic number 2. Scientific essentialism thus requires that philosophers distinguish clearly between semantic issues, epistemological issues and ontological issues.

Realistic analysis is the kind of analysis that should result when these and other fundamental distinctions are clearly recognized and rigorously maintained: distinctions between properties and predicates, natural kinds and arbitrary classes, species and instances, causal processes and mere sequences of events, essential and accidental properties and so on. That is, the programme of analysis should pay due attention to all of the important distinctions between kinds of objects, properties and processes existing in the world, their instantiations and their metaphysical interconnectedness. It is not good enough to treat properties or natural kinds as sets of abstract objects, or to think and reason about them as if they were nothing more than this. Realistic analyses are required which keep track of the universals as well as their instances.

I envisage, for example, the development of a realistic logic of chemistry that will not only explain instance reasoning, but do something to help us sort out the complex reasoning processes that were involved in the early development of chemical theory, for the history of chemistry provides an excellent case study in natural kinds reasoning. The chemical elements and compounds constitute the most readily accessible system of natural kinds of substances, their properties are mostly their essential properties, and the processes they undergo in chemical interactions are all natural kinds of processes that display the essential properties of the substances involved. The question is, how should we reason about and develop our knowledge of such a system? A logic of chemical theory that did justice to the complexities of the subject matter, and which chemists themselves would find useful, would be a significant step in the right direction.

The philosophy of mind

The American philosopher Wilfrid Sellars (1963) speaks of two very different images of reality. He calls them the "manifest" and the "scientific" images. The manifest image is the view of ourselves, the world and our place in it that derives from common experience, and from critical reflection on that experience. The scientific image is the view of reality that derives from science, when its laws and theories are understood realistically. The two images are seemingly incompatible. The scientific image, as it is presented to us by scientific realists, is of an objective world that consists of passive things pushed or pulled around by the forces of nature; the other, the manifest image, is one of a world inhabited by active things with intrinsic causal powers. The contrast is most striking in the case of the scientific and manifest images of ourselves. We are indeed pushed and pulled around by the forces of nature, but we are also capable of deliberating and acting freely within these constraints.

The most common response of seventeenth- and eighteenth-century philosophers to this problem was to divide the world into mental and physical components. Mental events were thought to be essentially different from physical events, to occur in different substances and occupy different realms. Science was taken as providing a description of the physical world, but not of the world of our experience. We are ourselves not even present in the scientific picture, they thought. The scientific account of reality would include descriptions of our bodies, and their movements, but it could not also include descriptions of our minds, our inner selves, or our experiences.

Such dualism did not solve the problem. If the material universe consisted of one kind of substance (having the primary characteristics of matter in a mechanistic world), but the human mind was made of a different kind of substance (having the capacities for experiencing, thinking, deciding, willing and so on), then what is the relationship between the two? How can physical events produce mental events (e.g. in perception), or mental events produce physical ones (e.g. in acts of will)? In which domain do the answers to these questions lie? Dualism thus created at least as many problems as it solved. It removed the need to provide a mechanistic theory of mind, but it provided no hint of an alternative theory that would explain how mental processes are related to the mechanisms of the body.

Dualism may not be acceptable, but the scientific image, as it is presented to us by scientific realists today, is also unacceptable, for it presents what is still essentially a Humean view of causation, and it has no natural place within it for many of those most human qualities and capacities that inform the manifest image we have of ourselves as rational agents, observing and responding to each other, and to the world around us. So the big question is, how can these two very different images of reality be reconciled?

Of all of the problems of philosophy, this is perhaps the most intractable. It cannot be solved just by focusing on the manifest image and attempting to articulate it. Nor can it be solved by resolutely attending to the nature of scientific enquiry, and ignoring its relationship to ordinary human experience. The two images must somehow be brought together, so that each can be seen in relation to the other, for what it is. The scientific image is far too powerful to be dismissed as a fabrication, with no implications for our conception of ourselves. On the other hand, the particular scientific image that has dominated Anglo-American philosophy since the eighteenth century seems too bare and passive to yield a satisfactory account, even of causation. And it is manifestly inadequate to provide a sound basis for understanding human agency, consciousness or experience.

The new essentialism has a significant contribution to make to the solution of this problem. The scientific image, as it has traditionally been portrayed by philosophers, is much more impoverished than it needs to be, for it represents what is still really an eighteenth-century view of the world. It does this by portraying inanimate nature as intrinsically passive, and therefore as being *prima facie* incapable of acting, except under the influence of external forces.[20] To bring the two images closer together, the scientific image needs to be updated. Specifically, it has to be recognized that the natural world is not intrinsically passive, but essentially active. It is a world in which all things have causal powers, and are therefore agents of one kind or another. So the power of agency is not something unique to human beings, or other living creatures. It is a pervasive feature of reality. This is not to say that human agency is not something rather special; it clearly is. On the other hand, it is not as alien to the essentialist's view of the world as it is to the Humean one.

Most philosophers today still believe, as Hume did, that the question of what causes what ultimately depends on what universal regularities hold. Their theory of causation thus makes it very difficult for them to account for human agency. If they are right, then our conscious decision-making processes, and the actions that we say stem from them, must all be understood in terms of regularities, constant conjunctions and the like, concerning which we, as conscious beings, can be nothing other than introspective spectators. But this is clearly not how they are in the manifest image. We do not see ourselves as being in such a passive role. Rather, we see ourselves as acting, and doing things for reasons. We see our processes of deliberation as ones that are thoroughly under our control, and which we can continue, suspend or eventually act upon. Acceptance of a Humean theory of causation thus makes it very difficult for anyone even to suggest a plausible theory of human agency.

More recent accounts of causation to be found in the writings of analytic philosophers are not, of course, all the same as Hume's. But most such theories of causation depend on analyses that bear a strong family resemblance to Hume's, for they are mostly agreed that a case of causation is ultimately just an instance of a universal generalization. They disagree with each other mainly about the nature and status of this generalization. More importantly, from our point of view, *they all cast the agent into the role of spectator to his or her own decision-making processes.* For an essentialist, however, agency is not a surprising or inexplicable phenomenon. On the contrary, everything is an agent of one kind or another. Everything has causal powers, and everything is capable of exercising its powers.

---

20. Internal forces are really just external forces acting between the parts of things.

The new essentialism thus brings a new perspective with it. For an essentialist, all effects are displays of causal powers, or due indirectly to such displays (as is the darkening of the room when the blinds are pulled). And these effects are not just events that happen to follow the triggering of causal powers; they are their manifestations, or at least the consequences of their manifestations. If the mousetrap is not set off by the taking of the cheese, then presumably the disturbance was not enough to release the causal power latent in the spring. Unless there are extraordinary defeating circumstances, there can be no question of the catch being released and the mousetrap not snapping shut. Such an unlikely event could only occur if something were to intervene to prevent the mousetrap snapping shut. In the absence of any such defeaters, the mouse will be a dead mouse.

Of course, the most elementary kinds of things all have fixed causal powers; that is, their dispositional properties are all fixed by their essential natures. A copper atom, for example, has the same dispositional properties wherever or whenever it might occur. The same is true of a proton or an electron. In Chapter 2 (p. 28) we called such kinds "fixed natural kinds". Their distinguishing feature is that you cannot change any of their dispositional properties. They just do what things of these kinds always have to do in the circumstances, and you cannot train them, or make them do anything else. There can be no question of a copper atom, for example, being disposed to behave in one way at one time, but in a different way at another time. Nothing with such variable powers could possibly be a copper atom.

However, more complicated things generally have variable causal powers. Even some things that are members of natural kinds have variable causal powers. In Chapter 2 (p. 28), we called these kinds of things "variable natural kinds". A piece of iron, for example, is plausibly a member of a natural kind, the members of which are all essentially crystalline structures of metallic iron. But pieces of iron can become fatigued, and hence brittle, or they may become magnetized, and hence acquire a capacity to attract other pieces of iron, generate electric currents and so on. So pieces of iron may gain or lose causal powers, depending on their histories or circumstances. Moreover, some things evidently have the capacity to change the dispositional properties of other things. A bar magnet, for example, has the capacity to magnetize another piece of iron. A radioactive substance has the capacity to effect changes of various kinds in things in its vicinity, including changes of their dispositional properties.

At the next stage of organizational complexity, it seems that things may not only be made to acquire or lose dispositional properties by the exercise of extrinsic causal powers, as the case of a bar magnet magnetizing another piece of iron well illustrates, but they may also be made to acquire or lose dispositional properties by the exercise of certain other of *their own* causal powers, that is, by the exercise of what may be termed "meta-powers". In general, an object may be said to have meta-powers if it has a reflective power to change some of its own causal powers. Inevitably, anything having meta-powers must appear to have higher-order powers, or powers of control, for any object that has such powers must have a capacity for self-direction.

It is plausible to suppose that human beings, and the members of all other advanced animal species, have acquired meta-powers of this kind in the process of evolution. Some of them may even have acquired meta-meta-powers, or powers of control of higher orders. If so, then human deliberation and action can fairly readily be explained. When someone acts to do something, they display a certain, perhaps very temporary, disposition. In at least some cases, this disposition results from an internal process of deliberation, a process that always involves the exercise of meta-powers. A deliberate action is not just an event of a kind that regularly happens to follow when intentional states of mind of a certain kind come into being. It is something that is done *by the agent* as a result of an intentional state of mind that is itself brought about by the agent, namely, by deliberation.

Thus, it seems that human beings not only have variable dispositional properties, as most complex systems have, but also meta-powers: *powers to change their own dispositional properties.* Other animals, no doubt, have similar meta-powers, but that such powers exist, and are exercised, seems quite evident from our own case. We exercise such meta-powers whenever we deliberate about what to do, and we call any action that may result from such a process a deliberate act of will.

The new scientific essentialism thus promises to reshape the scientific image of mankind. It promises to do so in a way that will bring the scientific and manifest images of ourselves closer together, for it deals with one aspect of the apparent conflict between them by providing a scientific image of human agency that bears enough resemblance to its manifest counterpart for it to be taken seriously as telling us what human agency really is. If the new essentialism is accepted, then human agency could be accepted as the manifest image of actions brought about by people exercising their meta-causal powers: their powers of control.

If, as seems likely, human agency is the exercising of our meta-powers to alter our own dispositions to act in one way rather than another, then it follows that we must be able to monitor our own mental processes, including our thinking, believing, desiring and so on. That is, we must have a kind of second-order or meta-perception, or ability to know directly by experience something of what is going on in our own heads when we are engaged in any of these activities. The neuro-physiological basis for this meta-perception must be something like a meta-level neuro-physiological process that scans the first-order processes involved in our various mental activities, including, it seems, the activity of scanning. Consciousness, I would think, is just such a meta-level scanning process.

CHAPTER 8

Wider Implications

Introduction

The impact of the new essentialism in philosophy should be considerable, because a great deal of modern philosophy was conceived in response to the scientific revolution of the seventeenth century, and therefore in reaction to Aristotelianism. But essentialism requires an understanding of the nature of reality that is more akin to the Aristotelian one than to the mechanist philosophy of Descartes or Newton. It also points to the need for a new programme of analysis, new conceptions of necessity and possibility, and new foundations for modal logics.

The consequences outside philosophy are likely to be less dramatic, because philosophy has ceased to be the dominant force that it once was, and the perspective of modern essentialism is less alien to modern science than it would have been to the sciences of the eighteenth century. The idea that things are intrinsically disposed to behave as they do is already widely accepted in fields such as physics and chemistry. In fact, it is chemistry that has provided much of the initial motivation for developing essentialist theory. Consequently, there are few, if any, implications for chemistry that are not already accepted by working chemists, and those for physics tend to be in areas such as cosmology, where physical theory engages with fundamental questions of ontology.

There are implications for biology, however, although even in this area many of the lessons of essentialism have already been absorbed, for the Darwinian revolution of the nineteenth century was really a triumph for the thesis of substantial intrinsic determinism, which is an important element of essentialism. Darwin did not have an understanding of the genetic basis for the characteristics or traits of organisms. But he knew that the determining factors were somehow intrinsic to the organisms involved. Yet many biologists, especially those with backgrounds in philosophy, are still fighting ancient battles, and are strongly anti-essentialist. They fear that to concede ground to essentialism is to give credence to ancient and untenable Aristotelian theories about the fixity of species. The new essentialism has no such implications. It is not only compatible with Darwinian natural selection, but the kind of intrinsic determinism it implies is a necessary condition for its possibility.

In sociology, history, politics and other areas of the social sciences, the lessons of essentialism have yet to be absorbed, for social theory is polarized between theories of social determination, on the one hand, and libertarian theories of human freedom, on the other, both of which are fundamentally antipathetic to the idea of an evolved human nature being a significant factor in social evolution. The social determinists conceive of human nature as a social construct that is overlaid on a basic animal nature of primitive desires and aversions. They argue that we are capable of being moulded by historical and economic forces to adapt to the kind of society in which we happen to find ourselves, and of internalizing the value system that is required to live in such a society. The libertarians likewise accept our animal natures as given, but consider that we also have a unique capacity to exercise freedom of choice. They argue that freedom of choice is a necessary condition for human well-being, and consequently that any restriction of human freedom of choice is bad, and can only be justified if it is necessary to increase the freedoms of others.

Thus, social scientists of all persuasions have been inclined to downplay the role of nature in the nature–nurture debate. For the social determinists, the biological evolution of social imperatives came virtually to a full stop when human beings came into existence. Thereafter, our attitudes and characters were moulded by social forces, as Marx is thought to have explained. For the libertarians, freedom of choice is a gift of God, or, at any rate, an inexplicable metaphysically obscure capacity that is definitive of our natures, and which cannot be denied. However, neither view is compatible with the new essentialism, for the new essentialists are not likely to think that biological evolution had no significant influence on human values, or on how human beings think and interact. On the contrary, most will think it very likely that our primitive value system evolved in unique ways to meet our needs. Specifically, it must have evolved to enable us to learn a language, and to live together and survive as tribal animals, despite our relative physical weaknesses. The problem is to find out more precisely what influences natural selection did have, and to construct a social framework within which our natural values can be adequately expressed, without otherwise undesirable consequences. Almost certainly, the libertarians are right to this extent: we do have a natural value of freedom of choice, which is intrinsic to our natures, and cannot be permanently suppressed. The history of liberation struggles is powerful evidence for this proposition. Presumably, the value of freedom was selected in the process of evolution to generate the creativity that is required for the survival of a tribe of animals that must live mainly by its wits. But perhaps there are other explanations. On the other hand, it is also clear that we are social animals, and that we have a primitive sense of justice or fairness that extends to all of those whom we consider to be members of our own tribe. Presumably, this value was selected to provide a basis for the social cohesion that any tribe must have to meet external threats. Biologically, therefore, it must be contrary to human nature, and so unsustainable, to stress either of these values at the expense of the other.

The fundamental questions for essentialists are likely to be: (1) what are our basic human values, and (2) how do they operate to generate our belief and attitudinal systems, and hence the kinds of social structures we have? An essentialist is likely to deny that we freely choose our own basic values, as a libertarian might think, or that we are socially constructed by the forces of history, as a Marxist might suppose. They would say, rather, that the most probable explanation of the origin of our values is that they were genetically encoded in the natural selective processes of evolution. Therefore, we should expect our most primitive human values, whatever they might be, to have survival value for humans living in the kinds of tribal societies in which we must originally have evolved. There are, for example, likely to be some primitive epistemic values that underpin our language-learning abilities and our reasoning processes, and some social values that favour tribal cohesion and cooperation in the struggle for survival.

Economics is a social science of a different kind, and many will argue that it is more akin to physics than to any of the other social sciences. Some would even say that the laws of neo-classical economics are laws of nature that describe how markets must behave in the absence of disturbing influences. Many of its founders certainly believed this to be the case. They did not take economics to be an experimental or inductive science, like chemistry or anthropology, but a theory of the same family as geometry or rational mechanics, which, at the time, were considered to be legitimate a priori sciences. The founders of the discipline thus supposed the appropriate methodology for economics to be a deductive one, and they thought its ultimate support must lie in the self-evidence of its axioms. Here is a quotation from Leon Walras:

> The pure theory of economics is a science which resembles the physico-mathematical sciences in every respect . . . The mathematical method is not an experimental method; it is a rational method . . . The physico-mathematical sciences do go beyond experience as soon as they have drawn their type concepts from it. From real-type concepts, these sciences abstract ideal-type concepts which they define, and then on the basis of these definitions they construct *a priori* the whole framework of their theorems and proofs. After that they go back to experience not to confirm but to apply their conclusions.   (1874: 71)

Essentialists tend to think that Walras was right about this. Most would argue that neo-classical theory has a status similar to that of Euclidean geometry. But, unlike their nineteenth-century counterparts, they conclude from this that pure economic theory has no more claim to be representative of the real world of economic transactions than any other formal theory. Economists themselves, however, seem to be less clear about this, and sometimes appear to be stuck philosophically in the nineteenth century, for they persistently speak as though they believed the real economy to be a pure free-market economy that is variously encumbered by taxes, distorted by government interference and rendered inefficient by trade unions and unnecessary transactions costs. The new essentialists see no reason to support this view. Market transactions are not natural kinds of processes that we might seek to describe in their pure and unsullied form. The pure and unsullied form that economists envisage is a political ideal, and not a purely theoretical one. The political ideal represents the kind of market that deeply committed libertarians would really like to see, and not an underlying reality, for there is, in fact, no such underlying reality. Market transactions in the real world are deals done by ordinary human beings for all sorts of reasons, from many different kinds of motives, and not the imperfect outcomes of what are fundamentally natural kinds of processes.

The influence on physics

As might be expected, metaphysical systems have profoundly influenced the directions of physical theory. The influences of Pythagoreanism on Kepler, of the theology of occasionalism on Newton, and of positivist thinking on Einstein, are all well documented. There are many other such examples. But there is probably no better illustration of the power of metaphysics to influence the directions of physical theory than the roles of the Leibnizian and Newtonian conceptions of reality in the development of the concept of energy.

1

According to mechanism, genuine causal powers are either non-existent (Hume), and therefore to be explained away (e.g. as illusory), or else they are derived from the agency of God (Newton, Berkeley). According to Leibniz, inanimate things have, or can acquire, causal powers. He called them "living forces" or *vires vivae*. While, strictly speaking, Leibniz did not believe in causal interactions as modern essentialists do – everything happens in Leibniz's theoretical world as a result of a pre-established harmony – he nevertheless believed that the *vis viva* of a body is the true measure of its effectiveness in causal interactions.

In Leibniz's philosophy *vis viva* (= mv^2, where m = mass and v = velocity) was thought of as the force that animates things in nature. He thus distinguished his own conception of force sharply from Newton's concept of "*vis mortua*". For Newton, forces are actions *externally* impressed upon bodies that are productive of changes of motion (i.e. changes of momentum). Hence, according to Newton, the correct measure of the force impressed upon a body is just the change in momentum that it undergoes: the quantity mv. Throughout the eighteenth century, the question of which is the true measure of force, mv^2 or mv, was hotly disputed. This dispute was not, as d'Alembert says it was, just a dispute about words.[21] It was an

---

21. This claim was made by D'Alembert in 1743 in his *Traité de Dynamique*. For an English translation of the relevant passage, see Magie (1935: 55–8). Laudan (1968) argues that, by taking an even-handed stance on the issue of the true measure of force, and arguing that the dispute was really only about words, D'Alembert (1743) did not finally settle the *vis viva* controversy, as many have supposed, for very few natural philosophers of the period thought that the dispute was just about words. It

absolutely fundamental disagreement about the sources of power in the world.[22] Do the laws of nature operate on an essentially passive world, as Descartes, Newton and Malebranche believed, or are the things in the world animated by living forces, as Leibniz believed?

Historically, this argument between the Leibnizians and the Newtonians about the sources of power was not just philosophical by-play. It was a debate within the natural philosophical (i.e. the scientific) community, engaged in by people who were themselves primarily natural philosophers; and it almost certainly had a major influence on the course of science itself. For Newton, forces are *actions* exerted upon bodies which are productive of changes of motion ("momentum" in today's terminology). As actions, forces are always *external* to the bodies they act upon, and are necessarily produced by objects, or beings, capable of exerting them. But if inanimate brute matter is intrinsically inert, as most philosophers of the time, including Newton, believed, then the source of their motion must lie elsewhere. They have to be pushed or pulled around by *agents* of some kind. Forces can only measure the strength of this pushing or pulling.

For Leibniz, forces are effectively *causal powers*. They may be either inherent causal powers, like gravitation, or they may be causal powers acquired by motion. In either case, forces are clearly located in the material world, and have no dependence, direct or indirect, on agency. Leibniz argued (reasonably, it now seems to us) that it takes as much force (read "causal power") to raise a weight of one pound through four feet as it does to raise four weights, each of one pound, through one foot. Conversely, he argued that the force acquired by a

---

is true that the intensity of the controversy diminished in the decades following D'Alembert's publication. Nevertheless, the controversy did continue throughout the century, and, if there was a developing consensus that the dispute was dead, this was only because the supporters of *vis mortua* (i.e. momentum) as the true measure of force believed that they had won the argument.

22. The case for this is powerfully argued by Iltis, who claims that the Leibnizian–Newtonian controversy reflected in the Clarke–Leibniz correspondence "was fundamentally a clash of philosophical world views on the nature of God, matter, and force" (1973: 343).

The Newtonian and Leibnizian groups of the 1720s developed a commitment to the mother scheme and took on the task of defending that system against the perceived threats of outside attacks. . . . They were unwilling and *unable* to see that the other side had valid arguments. The early *vis viva* controversy of the 1720s was therefore the result of a problem of communication brought about by the inability of the participants to cross the boundary lines of their particular natural philosophies. (1973: 344)

weight of four pounds falling through one foot must be the same as that acquired by a weight of one pound falling through four feet (as indeed it must be if force is *vis viva*).

To us, this may seem both true and obvious. Nevertheless, the concept of *vis viva* was firmly rejected by Newton, and by most natural philosophers in the eighteenth century. Indeed, rather than admit the basic significance of Leibniz's concept of *vis viva*, some of Newton's followers went to what may now seem to be quite extraordinary lengths to avoid having to use it in explanations.[23] By the end of the eighteenth century, the Newtonians were considered to have won this debate, although the reasons why they did so have never been entirely clear. Whatever the reason, the triumph of the Newtonians over the Leibnizians in natural philosophy is probably one of the main reasons why neither the dynamical theory of heat, nor the law of conservation of energy, for which the concept of *vis viva* is obviously central, were developed in the late eighteenth or early nineteenth centuries, when they clearly could have been.[24]

In his remarkable paper "Remarks on the Forces of Inorganic Nature", J. R. Mayer (1842) argued for the principle that has since become known as the law of conservation of energy. This paper owed much to the revival in Germany in the 1820s and 1830s of the Leibnizian tradition. Mayer argued that forces are one of just two species of causes: things which are able to change form, but remain quantitatively the same throughout the process of doing so, so that the principle, *causa aequat effectum*, is satisfied. The other kind of cause, he said, is matter, for matter, too, can undergo transformations while remaining quantitatively the same. Forces are distinct from matter, however, in that they lack such qualities as weight and impenetrability. Forces, he said, are *"indestructible, convertible imponderable objects"*, but "so far as experience goes", he said, "[matter and force] never pass one into another". The conceptual unification of mass and energy was thus anticipated approximately one hundred years before it was so disastrously demonstrated by the atomic bomb.

---

23. See Laudan (1968) for examples.
24. In fact, Sir Henry Cavendish did explore the possibility of a dynamical theory of heat, based on Leibniz's concept of *vis viva*, in the late eighteenth century, and wrote a draft treatise on the subject. Unfortunately, Cavendish did not finish rewriting his draft, and his treatise was not published in his lifetime. It was buried among other papers, and did not surface again until the late 1960s. See McCormmach (1988).

Mayer went on to argue that "falling force", or what we should now call "gravitational potential energy", and heat are both forces, and that any given quantity of either must therefore be equal to the quantity of *vis viva* into which it could in principle be transformed, or from which it could in principle be derived. He then used some old data on the specific heats of gases at constant pressure and at constant volume to calculate how much heat is required to cause the expansion of the gas at constant pressure. Thus he was able to calculate, correctly in principle, the mechanical equivalent of heat.

It is inconceivable that this paper could have been written by a Newtonian. The conceptual framework required for it is completely at odds with Newtonianism. On the Newtonian conception of force, Mayer remarked:

> Gravity being regarded as the cause of the falling of bodies, a gravitating force is spoken of, and so the notions of *property* and of *force* are confounded with each other: precisely that which is the essential attribute of every force – the union of indestructibility and convertibility – is wanting in every property: between a property and a force, between gravity and motion, it is therefore impossible to establish the equation required for a rightly conceived causal relation. If gravity be called a force, a cause is supposed which produces effects without itself diminishing, and incorrect conceptions of the causal connexion of things are thereby fostered. In order that a body may fall, it is no less necessary that it should be lifted up, than that it should be heavy or possess gravity; the fall of bodies ought not therefore be ascribed to their gravity alone.   (1842: 199, original emphasis)

Most philosophers nowadays would admit the legitimacy of both the Newtonian and Leibnizian concepts of force. They are both powerful tools for the analysis of dynamical systems. But in the eighteenth and early nineteenth centuries most natural philosophers thought they had to choose between them.

2

It is evident that the causal powers of things stretch out somehow beyond their boundaries. If the world were a Newtonian world of atoms in empty space, it would be mysterious how one object could affect another without mediation. According to Newton, whose authority on questions of natural philosophy dominated the eighteenth century, all causal power derives from God. It does not reside in matter, as many later Newtonians came to believe. So, if one object acts on, or is attracted by, another, this is not because of the intrinsic natures of these objects. Ultimately, it is because this is what God commands.

In a much-quoted letter to Bentley, in February 1692, Newton said:

> It is inconceivable that inanimate brute matter should, without the mediation of something else which is not material, operate on and affect other matter without mutual contact, as it must be if gravitation, in the sense of Epicurus, be essential and inherent in it. And this is one reason why I desired you would not ascribe innate gravity to me. That gravity should be innate, inherent, and essential to matter, so that one body may act upon another at a distance through a *vacuum*, without the mediation of anything else, by which their action and force may be conveyed from one to another, is to me so great an absurdity that I believe that no man who has in philosophical matters a competent faculty of thinking can ever fall into it. Gravity must be caused by an agent acting constantly according to certain laws, but whether this agent be material or immaterial I have left to the consideration of my readers.   (Thayer 1953: 54, original emphasis)

A modern essentialist answer to the problem of action at a distance is not to deny the reality of the causal powers, but rather to deny the absoluteness of the visual and tactile boundaries of things, for we now know that the visual and tactile boundaries of things are determined primarily by their electromagnetic powers, and not their very much weaker gravitational ones. Accordingly, it should not be too surprising to learn that material things do, in fact, stretch out beyond their visual boundaries, and so become engaged in causal processes that may involve action at a great distance. The distortion of space-time, which, according to general relativity, is "produced" by the presence of a heavy object, is not, we should say, an effect of its presence, but an integral and essential part of its being, without which the object could not exist. The distortion of the surrounding electromagnetic field within which an electron is (roughly) located is likewise not something that exists independently of the electron. Plausibly, electrons *just are* discontinuities of some kind in the electromagnetic and gravitational fields that we say they generate.

3

It is not clear what the implications of essentialism for modern physics will be. That will be for the physicists to tell us eventually. But there is one implication, at least, that seems likely to have an influence on the direction of theoretical enquiry. Presented with an intrinsic dispositional property, such as a radioactive decay propensity, a Humean is likely to look for an underlying categorical basis, for it is unacceptable to anyone who thinks as a Humean does that there should be any such real property.

One strategy, which we may call the Bohmian one, would be to try to explain the manifest statistical laws by reference to hidden variables whose measures may be assumed to have the corresponding statistical distribution. But this does not now seem to be a very hopeful strategy for, say, the propensity of a neutron to decay. Another strategy, which we may call the Everettian one, would be to postulate a bifurcating world, with divisions of the space-time manifold occurring at every point at which there is a quantum-mechanically indeterminate event, for this should enable the statistical laws that are to be explained to be understood simply as properties of the multiply-divided space-time manifold. But, to an essentialist, this strategy must appear to be grossly extravagant, for what is wrong with simple propensities? It is true that we cannot represent them easily in our imaginations. We could, perhaps, colour fundamental particles somehow according to their half-lives, if we really wanted to be able to visualize their different decay propensities. But visualization has no special value, except as an aid to thought, and what possible value could there be in representing the points along the world-line trajectories of radioactive particles as the loci of bifurcating worlds?

Essentialism in biology

According to the strict criteria of modern essentialism, biological species are not natural kinds. It is true that members of the same species have genetically similar constitutions, and that the kinds of genetic constitutions that are characteristic of a species form a more or less stable cluster. But co-specific animals or plants are rarely gen-identical, and the genetic make-up of the cluster of genotypes that is characteristic of a given species varies as evolution proceeds. The species classifications we make are thus dependent on what clusters of genetically similar organisms happen to exist in our era, and what genetically determined features we think are sufficiently salient to warrant distinctions of species.

Nevertheless, essentialist theory is undoubtedly relevant to biology. It is relevant methodologically, because essentialism requires us to distinguish between two kinds of causes: those of intrinsic origin, and those due to the imposition of external forces or constraints. Those of intrinsic origin are regarded as primary, and determinative of the basic nature of the effects to be explained. Those of external origin are considered to be secondary, and to result in modifications of the intrinsically determined outcomes. It is also relevant to the taxonomy of biological processes, and the explanation of their structure, for at least some of the processes described by biochemists and microbiologists do indeed belong to natural kinds, and the identities of these processes depend on the kinds of substances or structures involved in them, and on the chemical interactions that drive them. The cells, and cell structures, are natural kinds of things, and their processes of growth and reproduction are ordinary causal processes. Like causal processes in any area, they can be thwarted or interrupted, and appropriate conditions of heat, nutrition, environment and so on have to be met if they are to proceed. But the same is true of chemical processes generally, and there is no reason to think of microbiological or biochemical processes as being fundamentally different from the processes occurring in non-living matter.

But even if the biological systems we are dealing with are not, strictly speaking, natural kinds, they will often be sufficiently similar in their constitutions, and exhibit sufficiently similar patterns of behaviour, for explanations of the sorts characteristic of the physical sciences to be discoverable. The assumptions from which such explanations proceed will not, even if true, be necessarily true, if the kinds of events or processes to be explained are not natural kinds. Nevertheless, the postulates we make about the intrinsic natures of the things concerned in these processes might well, as a matter of fact, be true of the kinds of things that actually exist in the world. And if this is so, then we may well be able to explain why things of these kinds must behave as they do. They must behave as they do, because they are, in fact, constituted as they are, and all things so constituted must behave in this sort of way. If the kinds we are dealing with are not natural kinds, however, we cannot go on to argue that things of these kinds must be constituted as we suppose, or else they would not be things of the kinds they are. That is, we cannot argue that things of these kinds must behave in these sorts of ways in every possible world.

By its methodological focus on intrinsic determination, the new essentialism is likely to strengthen the hand of Darwinists in their struggle with the forces of reaction, whether religious, social determinist or liberal, for the natural selection of a characteristic or trait would be impossible without a considerable degree of genetic determinism concerning that characteristic or trait. It is true that a characteristic or trait may be co-selected, along with another which is beneficial to organisms of the kind concerned, and so not selected on its own merits. But these are the details of the evolutionary history of an organism that need not concern us here. What is vital is that the role of genetic causation be recognized, and not swept under the carpet to protect our religious prejudices, vanity or political theory.

Religious fundamentalists should take no comfort from the new essentialism, for it is not only compatible with Darwin's theory of natural selection, but it is probably the only scientifically plausible theory of the genesis of the specific traits and characteristics of organisms that is. If their genetic constitutions were not significant factors in determining their manifest traits and characteristics, then evolution by natural selection would be impossible. Yet many Darwinists do not seem to know who their friends are. Dan Dennett, for example, mounts a scathing attack on modern essentialism, even in fields like chemistry. He does so, evidently in the belief that essentialist theory is somehow antipathetic to Darwinism. But it is not. Dennett is, no doubt, motivated to discredit the old Aristotelian idea of fixed species of organisms, each having its own specific essence. But modern essentialists have no wish to defend this ancient doctrine anyway, and do not try to do so. On the contrary, the cluster concept of species, which any sensible modern essentialist would defend, combines the kind of genetic determinism that Darwinism requires as a basis for selection with the variability of outcomes that is needed if evolution is to occur.

The extremes of politics, the Marxists on the left, and the *laissez-faire* capitalists on the right, both have much more reason than the Darwinists to be threatened by the new essentialism, for the new essentialism must reinstate the concept of human nature, and put natural constraints on the kinds of social engineering practices that are sustainable, without excessive use of force or propaganda. It implies, for example, that our nature is neither radically individual-istic, as the capitalist economy assumes, nor a historical or social construct, as the Marxists generally believe. It is very likely, rather, that we are neither selfish individualists, as classical economic theory depicts us as being, nor socially malleable creatures who can be programmed to live happily in a society in which individual freedoms are suppressed, as historical determinists believe.

Essentialism and social theory

Social scientists tend to be strongly anti-essentialist. They associate essentialism with just about everything that is bad in social theory and practice: with racism, social Darwinism, sexism, and other positions which play down the roles of culture, circumstances, education or oppression in the development of human capacities and the formation of character. However, the new essentialism is not to be identified with such attitudes, and does not imply any of these distasteful positions. What it implies depends on what genetic differences there are between people, what effects these differences have, and whether these differences have any significant correlations with the differences that we commonly recognize. There are, undoubtedly, some significant differences between the genetic constitutions of individuals that are relevant to whether, or how well, they are able to do various things, for there are many seriously debilitating genetic disorders, and it is undeniable that different people do have different intrinsic abilities. There are also bound to be some significant differences in the intrinsic abilities of different groups of people, for almost any common-sense basis of classification. But statistical correlations of this kind are rarely more than weak tendencies. In any case, most such differences are likely to be irrelevant to issues of social policy. So there is no need for an essentialist to embrace any very politically incorrect position. And, even if there were grounds for doing so, this would be only a prudential reason for rejecting essentialism. Essentialists who are defending politically incorrect positions can expect to be demonized or vilified. But this fact would be irrelevant to the correctness or otherwise of their positions.

Essentialists cannot dismiss psycho- or sociobiology altogether, as many theorists who see themselves as morally and socially progressive have wanted to do, for this would be to deny the relevance of natural selection to human thinking, reasoning, language abilities, conceptualization, socialization and so on, which would indeed be a very implausible position to take. People are certainly members of a

157

biological kind, and biological kinds are sufficiently like natural kinds to make it likely that some patterns of linguistic, social or mental development are inbuilt, and common to all, or nearly all, members of the species. Indeed, it would be surprising if there were no psychological or sociological traits that human beings have, *qua* members of the genetic cluster to which they belong. Other animals undoubtedly have some specific behavioural traits, and naturally interact with each other in certain specific ways. Why shouldn't we? Essentialists must therefore expect to find that there are natural ways of thinking, reasoning, language-learning, conceptualizing, socializing and so on, and that at least some of these are genetically determined, and specific to our species.

From the point of view of an essentialist, there is no reason to suppose that the groups of human beings that we commonly distinguish between constitute natural kinds, and few of them bear even a close resemblance to such kinds. The race distinctions, for example, are genetically very fine-grained, and the races merge one into another in such a way as to make these distinctions very dubious. Moreover, the statistically measurable performance differences between the races may well be due, wholly or partly, to the effects of different customs, education, levels of poverty, social discrimination, or any of a number of other factors. Biologically, one might expect to find some differences to have emerged between tribes of people who have, prehistorically, had to cope, for very long periods, with radically different environments. So the hypothesis that there are significant racial differences in intrinsic capacities or dispositions cannot be ruled out a priori, as some have hoped. An essentialist must remain open to persuasion on this point. The differences between the sexes, however, are much more clear-cut, and are certainly genetically based. Moreover, they are differences that are likely, prehistorically, to have been very relevant to a tribe's ability to survive in crisis situations. Therefore, one might reasonably expect to find some essential differences between men and women that are not just physical differences. For example, there might well be ontogenetic differences in the ways in which men and women are disposed to behave and think. The differences between the sexes in crime rates, learning patterns, ways of socializing, and capacities for spatial visualization all strongly suggest that this is so.

The main focus of essentialism in social theory should not, however, be concerned with sub-groups of the human species, but with the intrinsic capacities and dispositions of human beings generally, for the species itself is sufficiently like a natural kind for there to be significant natural tendencies to individual and group behaviour that we would do well to understand. Sociobiology should not, therefore, be bogged down in an acrimonious dispute about the origins of racial or sexual differences in behaviour or preferences, but deeply concerned with the manifest traits and dispositions of mankind generally. For example, it seems that we have a primitive need for security, which, in the absence of any substantial threat, may well become a paranoid drive for power. To satisfy this need, we are evidently disposed to admire and follow a strong and ruthless leader, if we perceive it to be in the interests of the power or security of the tribe to do so. Our whole history as a species testifies to our willingness to accept such a leader, and to act with the utmost barbarity in pursuit of his ambitions. War and genocide are not new phenomena, but as old as mankind itself. Therefore, the tendencies that lead to them, and make their execution possible, are presumably genetically encoded. Plausibly, the instinct to follow such a leader, and do his bidding, has to do with the imperative of tribal survival, although it sometimes seems to go well beyond that. Whatever its origins, its existence is hard to deny.

Social theorists had, therefore, better find some viable strategies for sublimating or diverting this instinct, given the fearsome destructive power of modern warfare. It is pointless to try to deny its existence, or even to suppress it, for if it is a natural tendency, as indeed it seems to be, it cannot be extinguished in the short term. In the tribal context in which the instinct to follow a powerful leader to destruction arose, there were no doubt reasons for its natural selection. But whatever they were, it is clear that they no longer exist. On the contrary, this disposition is now the greatest threat to our survival as a species.

The pattern of essentialist explanations

Essentialists seek to expose the underlying causes of things, and to explain why things are as they are, or behave as they do, by reference to these underlying causal factors. Consequently, explanations of the sort that essentialists are seeking must always have two parts. They must contain hypotheses about the underlying structures or causal powers of things, and hypotheses about how things having these structures and powers must behave in the specific circumstances in which they exist. The hypotheses we make about the underlying structures or causes of things constitute what, following Roy Bhaskar (1978), we might call the proposed "mechanism", although the mechanism need not be anything like a classical one. The proposed mechanism in any such explanatory framework is considered to be determined by the natures of the things concerned. Therefore, it is considered to be fixed and invariant. The circumstances of a thing's existence, on the other hand, are always contingent, and possibly variable. Consequently, this part of the explanation has a different status from that of the proposed mechanism.

The distinction between the underlying mechanism and the circumstances of its existence is also reflected in Imre Lakatos's methodology of scientific research programmes (Lakatos 1970), although Lakatos's reasons for introducing the concept had nothing to do with essentialism. The "hard core" of a scientific research programme defines what is believed by practitioners in the field to be the basic structure of the events that underlie the range of phenomena to be explained. It describes the accepted mechanism. The "protective belt" consists of a number of subsidiary theories or hypotheses, developed to explain the specifics of what occurs, or any anomalies that may arise from the core theory, or to extend the range of the basic theory to include explanations of any effects that cannot be explained satisfactorily on the basis of the hard-core assumptions alone. The "dark matter" hypothesis, for example, is one that has been proposed to deal with a certain anomaly in the relativistic Hot Big Bang theory of the origin of the universe, and so belongs to the protective belt that surrounds the core assumptions of this theory.[25] Van der Waals's equations of state are laws that belong to the protective belt of the kinetic theory of gases, for the theory from which they were derived is an extension, or modification, of the core kinetic theory. In this case, the extended theory was designed to deal with forces that were known to be operating, but were ignored in the original model.

Lakatos argued that the hard core of a research programme has a different status from that of its protective belt. It is not directly falsifiable, and it is held dogmatically. If what looks like counter-evidence comes to light, then research workers in the field must seek to adjust the protective belt, rather than abandon the core assumptions of the theory. This, at any rate, is normal practice. The core

---

25. The observable quantity of matter in the universe is very much less than it should be according to the theory.

assumptions will be questioned, only in desperation – for example, if the theory seems to be failing in a number of different ways, or on many different fronts – to provide a satisfactory basis for explanation, for the test of the core assumptions is whether they can be defended from refutation by means that are methodologically satisfactory. Even then, the core assumptions will be abandoned only if a new mechanism can be proposed that promises to account for the phenomena better than the old one.

Although this pattern of explanation, and this kind of structuring of scientific research programmes, are accepted as normal and appropriate in the physical sciences, they are often regarded with suspicion in the human sciences. It is true that there are some respectable theories in these sciences that aim to explain just the basic structure of causation in their fields. Theoretical linguistics, for example, aims to develop a general theory of language structure and acquisition that is applicable to all human languages. Logic aims to develop a general theory of rationality adequate to explain the basic structure and dynamics of rational belief systems (Ellis 1979). Neo-classical economics aims to develop a general theory of the structure and dynamics of market economies. Within each of these disciplines there are research programmes characterized by hard-core assumptions and protective belts of hypotheses. But abstract model theories like those in theoretical linguistics, logic and economics are rare in the human sciences, and, for the most part, they are held to be inappropriate. A "hard core" set of assumptions in sociology, history or politics, for example, would be considered ideological, and therefore contrary to the ideal of objectivity in which practitioners of these disciplines implicitly believe (whether or not they think it is achievable).

The question therefore arises, when are the patterns of explanation and theory development that are characteristic of the physical sciences appropriate in a given area of study, and when are they inappropriate? When is it reasonable to assume that a general theory of causation in an area of study is possible? The answer that will be given here is: it is reasonable to believe that a general theory of causation in an area is possible only if the kinds of entities under investigation can reasonably be assumed to belong to natural kinds, and the causal processes involved in their actions and interactions can reasonably be supposed to be displays of the intrinsic causal powers, capacities, liabilities and so on of things of these kinds.

Economic essentialism

The social scientific theory that has most often been considered to be an objective science, and whose theorems might be said to be necessarily true, is neo-classical economics. It is widely believed, for example, that the neo-classical equilibrium postulate is necessary, and has the status of a law of nature, for the postulate is thought to describe what must, of necessity, be the case in any pure competitive market economy in equilibrium, and therefore to describe the state towards which any such economy must tend, if it is left to its own devices. Let us call this theory about the nature of economics "economic essentialism".

Economic essentialists believe that there is a positive science of economics that is comparable in status to physics, and that its laws have the same kind of necessity. It is a science, they would say, that differs from physics in subject matter, and in the kinds of observations that can be made. But it has a body of established high-level theory, just as physics has, a methodology that is similar, and a number of major research programmes under way. The methodology that is usually deemed to be appropriate to economics is Lakatosian. Consequently, economists now distinguish, as Lakatos did for research programmes in the physical sciences, between the "hard-core" assumptions, which define the programmes, and are held dogmatically, and the theories or hypotheses belonging to their protective belts, which are more open to empirical refutation.

However, economics is not fundamentally like physics, because the free markets of economic theory are not theoretical ideals, but political ones. The free market is not the underlying structure of any market economy, whatever the social customs of the society in which it is located, but the preferred structure of the theoretician. The reason is simply that market economies do not constitute a natural kind. There are markets, and market transactions, but these are social institutions or processes, not things or processes of kinds that exist in nature independently of human knowledge, language or customs. Nor are they sufficiently like natural kinds of things or processes to justify treating them as such, for they are not grounded in human nature, as one might reasonably expect, but in certain political ideals, namely, those of freedom and individualism.

Fundamentally, neo-classical economic theory is an abstract system of definitions and postulates that has no foundation in any underlying theory. It is not, for example, founded on studies of human psychology, which one might reasonably expect, given that it is so much concerned with human decision-making. You will search the literature in vain, however, if you look for an empirical or theoretical justification for the fundamental axioms of free-market economics. The theory has no such foundation in either psychology or sociology. Rather, neo-classical equilibrium theory is like Euclidean geometry, and its methodology is rationalist, as Leon Walras argued in the nineteenth century.

If Walras was right, however, and neo-classical economics is formally like a system of geometry, then the methodology of economics ought not to be Lakatosian. That is, economic theory should not be treated as though it were a theory about some underlying reality that deserves to be protected from direct refutation. If the axioms, definitions and postulates of economic theory involved assumptions about the fundamental nature of the things or processes involved in a natural kind of process, then there would indeed be a principled reason for treating these propositions as "hard-core" assumptions, and protecting them. However, there is no principled case for any such dogmatism about the assumptions of neo-classical economics, or for trying to absorb all clashes with experience into the protective belts of these theories, as many economists now suppose. On the contrary, economists should be wide open to the development of non-classical theories of market economies.

The neo-classical Walrasian programme in economics is similar to the nineteenth-century Euclidean programme in the theory of space and time. The Euclidean programme of Lorentz sought to explain the observable spatiotemporal properties of things in terms of a "hard core", consisting of a Euclidean geometry of space and time, and a "protective belt" made up of assumptions about universal forces: forces that are capable of distorting things in a uniform way, and uniformly retarding all sorts of clocks (Reichenbach 1928: Ch. 1). Neo-classical theory similarly defines an idealized kind of market, operated by ideally self-interested agents of a certain kind, and erects around it a protective belt of market-distorting forces that are capable of producing whatever effects may actually be observed. But there is no underlying natural process that this model is intended to describe, and the case for dogmatism about the assumptions of neo-classical economic theory is no better than that for dogmatism about the geometry of space and time.

A good case for Lakatosian dogmatism concerning hard-core assumptions exists if these assumptions are required by background theory. The theory of temperature radiation, for example, is grounded in quantum mechanics, and Planck's law of black body radiation is derivable from this background theory. Consequently, Planck's law is not an independent hypothesis that might easily be rejected. If the observed pattern of heat radiation from a given body did not conform to Planck's law, even though the body appeared to be black, then this would certainly present us with an anomaly, for Planck's law is a hardcore assumption of the theory of heat radiation, and physicists generally would be very reluctant to give it up. It is not an a priori truth, however, and, for all we know, it may eventually be shown to be false. But this could only happen if it could be shown somehow that its quantum-mechanical derivation was faulty. In the absence of any such proof, it would just remain an anomaly. Either the body in question is not really black, it would be said, or there is an undiscovered flaw in the proof.

A case for Lakatosian dogmatism might also exist if the supposed hard core of the theory described what we could reasonably suppose to be a natural kind of process: a kind of process that has a structure and a dynamic that exist objectively in the world independently of human knowledge, language or understanding. But such processes can exist only in the natural world, where the things taking part are themselves members of natural kinds. Molecular processes, for example, such as those postulated in the dynamical theory of heat, might reasonably be supposed to be ones that belong to natural kinds. Consequently, it may be reasonable to defend the hard core of the dynamical theory of heat by making adjustments, where necessary, to this theory's protective belt. But human beings have at least some culturally or socially determined characteristics that are relevant to how they are disposed to behave, and the market processes in which they are involved are not natural kinds of processes, but social interactions between human beings. Consequently, there is no reason to suppose that neo-classical economic theory describes an underlying natural kind of process.

This being the case, there is no reason to suppose that the appropriate methodology for economics is Lakatosian. On the contrary, the basic principles of economic theory should be as much open to question as any others, and a serious effort to construct non-classical economic theories is now urgently needed. Yet, most economists are evidently content to believe that their dogmatic attitudes to the fundamental tenets of neo-classical economics are methodologically justified. They are not.

The widespread acceptance of Lakatosian methodology as appropriate for economics leads to other errors, for it leads immediately to the view that there is a pure market economy that lies at the heart of every real one. This underlying pure economy is, however, beset by various non-market forces, subject to various social or political influences, and impeded by all sorts of frictions that had better be eliminated. The real economy is thus conceived to be hedged in and carrying all sorts of baggage, and so inefficient, and in need of a good overhaul. This overhauling process is known as "economic reform". It is false, however, that the market is a machine labouring under difficulties, and so failing to deliver the goods and services it should be delivering. There is no such machine, and the question of what role the market should have in a given economy is a political one. The free market, conceived as being a pristine engine, is as much a fiction as a Euclidean triangle. There is no such thing, except in the mind of the theorist.

Appendix

The following papers were presented at the annual conference of the Australasian Association for the History, Philosophy and Social Studies of Science held in Melbourne in June 2001. David Armstrong raises what he sees as being the two most serious difficulties for essentialism. He argues, first, that essentialism requires the existence of properties whose identities depend on the relations that their bearers must have to the possibly non-existent events that would constitute their displays. He does not claim that such properties cannot exist. But he does argue that if essentialism requires that there be such properties, then this is a serious problem for essentialists. This is Armstrong's Meinongian objection. The second difficulty is that presented by Richard Swinburne with his infinite regress argument. This is not, as Armstrong concedes, a problem for the version of essentialism defended in my two books on essentialism. But then, says Armstrong, my way of avoiding the problem leads to other problems about the nature of categorical properties. The discussion of these problems is taken up in my reply.

Two problems for essentialism

D. M. Armstrong

In his book *Scientific Essentialism* (2001), and in the draft of his new book *The Philosophy of Nature: A Guide to the New Essentialism*, Brian Ellis has told us a lot about the advantages, as he sees them, of his essentialist view. That is fine as far as it goes, but like most large projects in metaphysics there are serious difficulties to be addressed. I find this even with my own views. I will take up what I think are the two most serious problems for Ellis's position.

Consider the non-relational or, as some say, intrinsic properties of objects. Ellis and I agree that, as a matter of ontology, objects have such properties, and we agree that it is up to our best science, not to our semantics, to give us the catalogue of these properties. The central cases of these properties, he holds, are powers. They are powers to affect and be affected by other objects, *and there is nothing more to them than that.*

If, as Ellis does, you postulate that the work of the world is done by powers of this sort, then you seem to get the interesting result that, at least in a deterministic world, effects of causes will be necessary: absolutely, metaphysically, necessary. This is a very striking result, and may easily intoxicate you. But in metaphysics, as elsewhere, you have to pay for what you get. These power-properties are very strange beasts. A thing's powers persist, in normal cases, even when they are not manifesting themselves. So consider an object with one of these power-properties, but let it not be manifesting that property. (Perhaps it will never do so.) Still, this property contains within itself, or perhaps we should say points to, the manifestation that is not occurring. It is "ready to go" as Charlie Martin, who holds a similar theory, is wont to say. It is ready to go in a certain particular direction, and this readiness is of its essence. If it were not of the essence of the property, then there would be no necessity for the manifestation in the case where it *does* go. Another philosopher, George Molnar, who held a view even closer to Ellis's than Martin's is, was so impressed by this point that he spoke of such properties as having "physical intentionality".

Is one prepared to have such properties on the ground floor of one's ontology? I don't like the idea. It seems to smack of a Meinongian relation to the non-existent – in this case a relation to the manifestation that does not occur. That is the first of my two criticisms.

Ellis tries to answer this difficulty in §3.11 of *Scientific Essentialism*. His first move is to argue that causal powers, being characteristically quantitative, allow "one causal power to explain an infinite range of quantitatively distinct dispositions". In language that he does not use, but which I think is useful, he is saying that the powers are determinables, while "the quantitatively distinct dispositions" are the determinates falling under the determinable power. That seems to make his problem worse, not better. There is one particular manifestation of the power that is actually manifested in a particular situation, but a huge number of manifestations of that power will be empirically possible yet never occur. The power in the particulars points to all of these.

I think he is aware of this difficulty. He seems to try to meet it when he argues that causal powers essentially involve causal relations – the point, I take it, is that the relation (taken as a determinable, he seems to mean) has two terms – "not between particular events but between certain natural kinds of events". Suppose we allow this. That gets rid of Meinongianism at just one point. What advance is this? At the level of determinates, the "pointing to non-existents" of the causal powers persists.

Perhaps one can live with physical intentionality. That is what Molnar was prepared to do, and that would be my recommendation to Ellis. But the second difficulty is really serious. If the properties that make up the cause are pure powers, then the effects will have to be pure powers also, and the effects of the effects, and so on. In scholastic terms, where does potentiality get cashed out as act? Where do we arrive at some concrete nature, something that is other than mere power? Surely the world is not a matter of particulars that have nothing but pure powers, powers that are then shuffled around the particulars. That is unbelievable.

Now, as it stands, this is not Ellis's position. I think it applies to Sydney Shoemaker. Shoemaker seems to go out of his way to create this difficulty for himself by, apparently, urging that all those properties *and relations* that are taken ontologically seriously be treated as powers. At any rate, Richard Swinburne, debating with Shoemaker, raises just this difficulty for him.[26] Ellis, and Molnar before him, are both aware of the Swinburne problem and try to provide some stuffing, as it were, some non-power nature, for particulars by admitting a second class of properties alongside the pure powers. Molnar calls them "non-powers" which does well enough; I would call them categorical properties.

In *The Philosophy of Nature*, Ellis calls them "structural properties", and instances the structures of molecules, atoms and so on. It would appear that spatiotemporal relations between particulars are

---

26. See Sydney Shoemaker (1983) and Richard Swinburne (1983). See page 296 of Shoemaker (1983) for his remark that his account of properties "could be extended to relations as well as properties . . .".

structures in his sense. They are definitely not powers. And they are not epiphenomenal features of the world. As Ellis says in his new book, very well I think, "For every property must be capable of manifesting itself to us in some way or other – otherwise we could never know about it." It looks as though these structural properties must have some "causal role", in David Lewis's phrase. And will they not have that role contingently only? Not being powers, they do not necessitate any particular causal role.

As Ellis points out, structures ontologically depend upon the elements that are structured. No elements, no structure – although the elements could exist unstructured. I suspect that this encourages him to think that the power-properties can somehow "take account" of the structural properties in such a way that preserves the metaphysical necessity of the operation of the powers of the elements. I don't think this can be done.

Consider gravitational attraction between two masses in a Newtonian world, with mass taken as a power-property. The distance between the two objects determines the attractive forces generated. Different distances: different forces. The objects will have to be sensitive to the difference: they will have "know", so to speak, what forces to generate. How is that to happen without the distance being a causal factor? But distance is not a power. So it would seem to be contingent what its contribution is.

Ellis would want to say, I take it, that the powers bestowed by the masses are powers to attract according to the inverse square formula, which essentially involves distance. Are the distances epiphenomenal, then? No, Ellis says, they make their causal contribution. Very well, then will this contribution not be contingent? Then they might have made a different contribution. So the inverse square law is not necessary after all. You need a Shoemaker treatment of distances, making the distances into contributory powers, to get necessity.

You will see that I am putting a destructive dilemma to Ellis. Either every factor involved in a causal action is a power, and then the Swinburne objection kicks in; or else there are non-powers involved. If non-powers are involved, then their causal contribution is contingent. And then the effects will not be necessary.

In *Scientific Essentialism* (§3.12) Ellis tries to deal with this problem thus. He says that such properties as shape and size "are known to us because things of different shape and size affect us differentially". But then he goes on (limiting himself to shape), we do not think there must be a distinctive causal power for each different shape. The different shapes are reflected in the different patterns of sensory stimulation, and these different patterns arise, we suppose, from the different patterns of distribution of the causal powers in the world we are observing.

But the trouble with this is that "patterns of distribution" are not powers, and yet the particular pattern involved in the particular case *modifies* the operation of the powers. That is the causal role of the patterns. And it would appear to be a contingent role.

I do see one thing for Ellis to do here. He could simply claim that the causal role of the structural properties is as necessary as the operation of the powers. But this will be *ad hoc*. The simple argument that he has for the necessity of the operation of the powers will be quite lacking. That is a *transparent* necessity. Once an untransparent necessity is introduced into the theory, as the operation of the patterns of distribution are, where does the matter stop? For instance, why should I not revise my own theory and say that all properties are categorical, but the laws that connect the properties are necessary? That is a nice economical theory because it postulates only one type of property.

Response to Armstrong

Brian Ellis

David Armstrong presents me with a destructive dilemma:

> Either every factor involved in a causal action is a power, and then the Swinburne objection kicks in; or else there are non-powers involved. If non-powers are involved, then their causal contribution is contingent. And then the effects will not be necessary.

The Swinburne objection is this: if all of the properties and relations that are supposed to be real are causal powers, then their effects can only be characterized by their causal powers, and so on. So causal powers are never manifested. They just produce other causal powers in endless sequence. This is a difficulty for Sydney Shoemaker, I think, as Armstrong points out. But it is not one for me, since I am a believer in categorical properties: properties that have identities that are independent of their causal roles.

But then, says Armstrong, I am caught on the other horn of the dilemma. If categorical properties have identities that are independent of their causal roles, then they cannot have the causal roles they have of necessity. They can only have these roles contingently.

This ingenious argument rests on the assumption that the laws of action of the causal powers are not functions of the circumstances in which they act. If the effect on some A is a function of its distance D from a causal influence C, then Armstrong thinks that there are only two possibilities: either D is a contributing cause to the overall effect, which makes its contribution by necessity, or it is not. If it is, then I am caught up in Swinburne's regress. If it is not, then the distance must make its contribution contingently. However, there is another possibility. One can simply deny that D is a contributing cause. In my view, D is a dimension of the causal set-up. It is one of the categorical properties that both affects and, in this case, is also affected by, the causal power. Let me explain.

The causal powers all have laws of action that are of their essence, for, ontologically, a causal power is a relationship between an object (its bearer) and a natural kind of process (its display). Consequently, anything having a given causal power must be disposed to act as its law of action requires. The law of action of a given causal power describes the kinds of changes that must result when the causal power is activated in circumstances of the appropriate kind, for example, when an object having the power is placed in such circumstances. In the simplest cases, the laws of action of the causal powers do not refer to other causal powers. Rather, they offer categorical descriptions of the kinds of set-ups (the causal set-ups) in which they operate, and say how things must change as a result of their operation (the effects). The categorical properties of things thus enter into this account only as properties of the causal set-ups, or properties of the resulting, or changing, states of affairs. They are Hume's passive causes and effects. The powers are the drivers of the actions that occur.

Armstrong has two serious concerns about this account. Firstly, as Armstrong points out, a causal power might never be brought into an appropriate causal set-up, and so might remain forever dormant. Hence, the causal powers are potentialities, and in the limiting cases, pure potentialities, that is, there are no underlying structures to hold them. This is the basis for Armstrong's Meinongian worry, which I will come to. Secondly, my account makes essential use of categorical properties. But what account can an essentialist possibly give of properties that are not powers?

Let me address the second of these two worries first. For an essentialist, there are two main problems concerning categorical properties. The first is the knowledge problem. If categorical properties are not causal powers, then, it is argued, they cannot affect us. Therefore, we can never know about them. My answer to this worry is, briefly, that we know about categorical properties either directly by empirical observation, or indirectly by inference to the best explanation. I assume that realism about the observed structures of things is the only plausible position to take, for we must at least suppose that the actual world has structures formally similar to these. Further, I suppose that realism about the structures postulated in the most highly successful theories of physics and chemistry is likewise mandated. Otherwise the empirical successfulness of these theories would be inexplicable. Thus, for realism about categorical properties I simply rely on the usual arguments for scientific realism.

The second is the ontological problem. If categorical properties are not causal powers, then what are they, and how are they related to the causal powers? My answer to this question is, briefly, that categorical properties are structures of, or within, the bearers of causal powers. They are not themselves causal powers; nevertheless, causal powers of the kinds that actually exist could not exist without them. They could not exist, because most, if not all, causes are necessarily productive of changes to categorical structures. I do not endorse the mechanist doctrine that all changes are changes of position, orientation or the like. An electron–positron annihilation, for example, is not a mechanistic change. Nor is the spectral emission of a photon from an excited atom. But these are changes of categorical structures, nevertheless. My position is that all causation of the kind that actually occurs in this world necessarily results in changing categorical structures of one sort or another.

The essentialist ontology I have described includes both powers and structures. The powers are dispositional properties, and are readily identifiable by how they dispose their bearers to behave. The structures, on the other hand, are not powers, but frameworks of a kind that might well give shape or form to many different powers. Methane (CH_4), silane (SiH_4), and carbon tetrachloride (CCl_4) all have a tetrahedral structure. Nevertheless, these substances have different causal powers, due to the different causal powers of their constituent atoms. In this case, the common structure is spatiotemporal, and plausibly, if the same structure can exist in two or more different molecules, it might also exist in another world with other kinds of atoms – atoms that are unlike any that exist in this world. Therefore, it is plausible to suppose that some structural properties, for example, the spatiotemporal ones, might well exist in worlds other than the kind of world in which we live. If this is so, and the same structures may exist in worlds with different causal powers, then the structures are ontologically at least as fundamental as the powers, and are not dependent on them.

What then can we say about structures? They do not seem to be just causal powers, like those they inform. On the other hand, they must do something, or we could never know about them. I agree. They inform the structures in which the causal powers operate, the structures that result from their operation and, ultimately, the structure of our experience. Kant argued that space and time are pure forms of sensuous intuition, and so, like most of us, wished to distinguish between the content and the form of what is seen or heard. The spatial and temporal properties of observed events refer to their visual or tactile forms, he supposed; the observable qualities of things refer to their manners of affecting us.

An essentialist can agree that our knowledge of structures derives ultimately from the structure of experience, but an essentialist must hold that powers and structures would exist, even if there were no sensuous intuition. So an essentialist cannot accept the Kantian identification of space and time as pure forms of sensuous intuition. But perhaps an essentialist can say something a bit similar. For an essentialist, space and time should perhaps be considered to be the pure forms of physical structure. All causes and effects are events in space and time; so they are necessarily limited by the kinds of spatial and temporal relationships that can exist in our kind of world. Our theories of space and time should be seen as placing certain overall restrictions on what kinds of causal set-ups, and what kinds of effects, we may consider to be possible.

According to essentialism, structural properties neither add to, nor subtract from, the powers, but determine the structural frameworks within which the powers operate. They are the properties of the causal set-ups and the properties of the displays of the causal powers. There are laws of action of the causal powers, depending on the categorical properties of the circumstances in which they operate, and laws of distribution of the effects they produce, which are functions of the categorical properties of the systems they affect. The orbiting stars of a binary system go around each other in a certain complex way, and it is possible to describe how they do so without attempting to explain this effect. To explain it, we have to suppose that there are causal powers that operate in a certain way, depending on the relative masses, distances, velocities and directions of motion of the stars. The law of distribution of effects is thus explained by reference to the structures and powers, and the laws of action of the powers, which together are supposed to be adequate to produce these effects. But note that the structural causes are postulated to explain the structuring of the effects.

The general rule is that structures require structures to explain them, and powers require powers. Powers alone cannot explain structures, nor structures powers.

The following picture thus emerges. There are causal powers that operate to produce various kinds of effects. Effects of the kinds they produce are normally structured, that is, they have a kind of dimensionality, in that they may be greater or less in any of a number of different respects, apparently independently of each other. To explain such a complex dimensional structure in the range of possible effects, it is necessary to suppose that the causal powers, or the set-ups within which they operate, also have a certain dimensionality. Specifically, they must have dimensionalities that are at least equal to that of the ranges of their possible effects. The categorical properties of things, I suggest, may thus be identified as the dimensions of the powers, or of the set-ups within which they are embedded.

Further, if I am right in speculating that they are properties that could exist unchanged in worlds that have other causal powers, then we might identify the categorical properties simply as those that could exist in a Humean world: a world without causal powers.

Armstrong's Meinongian objection concerns my willingness to embrace pure potentialities, that is, properties whose identities depend entirely on what they dispose their bearers to do, and that, in themselves, are nothing more than this. Such properties, Armstrong says, are Meinongian, for, consider the case of an object with a dormant causal power: one that is not currently being manifested, and perhaps never will be. Such a power would seem to be nothing in itself. It has no categorical basis, and it does nothing other than "point to" how it would be manifested if the circumstances in which the object existed were different – circumstances that are not, and perhaps never will be, realized.

It is true that if one is looking for the structure of a pure power, then one will look in vain. But I do not see that structures have ontological priority. It is true that one cannot visualize an intensional magnitude, such as a causal power normally is, unless one thinks of it as brighter, or more intense in some other way. But what is visualizable does not seem to be important. For my part, I am happy enough to accept the non-visualizability of causal powers.

Given the kind of ontology developed in *Scientific Essentialism*, causal powers do not seem to be so very different from other properties. They are generic universals that are instantiated in the objects that possess them, as all genuine properties are. Their instantiations are not necessarily manifest to us. To manifest a causal power it is necessary to cause it to be displayed. But the same it true of any universal. To make any instance of a structural universal manifest to us it is necessary to cause it to be displayed somehow, say, by shining a light on it, or bombarding it with X-rays.

Consider Berkeley's tree in the quad, which we will suppose has never been seen, and never will be seen. Let us, furthermore, isolate it causally, so that it never affects, and is never affected by, anything else in the universe. Does it have shape and size? My answer is: yes, of course. But do the shape and size of the tree exist only as potentialities? Do they, as it were, "merely point to" their possible manifestations? Or would the shape and size of the tree become realities only if, counter-factually, the tree were somehow brought out of its isolation and revealed to us? No. Then what about its colour? Does its colour exist although no one has ever seen it? Yes it does. Then, finally, what about its inertial mass? Does its inertial mass exist, although the tree has never been accelerated? Why not? Why should what requires illumination to be made manifest have priority over what requires acceleration?

Bibliography

Armstrong, D. M. 1978. *Universals and Scientific Realism*, 2 vols. Cambridge: Cambridge University Press.

Armstrong, D. M. 1983. *What is a Law of Nature?* Cambridge: Cambridge University Press.

Armstrong, D. M. 1997. *A World of States of Affairs*. Cambridge: Cambridge University Press.

Ayers, M. R. 1981 "Locke versus Aristotle on Natural Kinds", *The Journal of Philosophy* 78, pp. 247–72.

Backhouse, R. E. 1993. "Lakatosian Perspectives on General Equilibrium Analysis", *Economics and Philosophy* 9, pp. 271–82.

Bealer, G. 1987. "The Philosophical Limits of Scientific Essentialism", in *Philosophical Perspectives 1*, J. Tomberlin (ed.), pp. 289–365. Atascadero: Ridgeway.

Bhaskar, R. 1978. *A Realist Theory of Science*. Hassocks, Sussex: Harvester Press.

Bigelow, J. C. 1990. "The World Essence", *Dialogue*, 29, pp. 205–17.

Bigelow, J. C. 1999. "Scientific Ellisianism", in *Causation and Laws of Nature*, parts I and II, H. Sankey (ed.), pp. 56–76. Dordrecht: Kluwer Academic Publishers.

Bigelow, J. C. and Pargetter, R. J. 1990. *Science and Necessity*. Cambridge: Cambridge University Press.

Bigelow, J. C., Ellis, B. D. and Lierse, C. 1992. "The World as One of a Kind: Natural Necessity and Laws of Nature", *British Journal for the Philosophy of Science* 43, pp. 371–88.

Burtt, E. A. 1932. *Metaphysical Foundations of Modern Science*, 2nd edn. London: Routledge and Kegan Paul.

Carroll, J. W. 1994. *Laws of Nature*. Cambridge: Cambridge University Press.

Cartwright, N. 1983. *How the Laws of Physics Lie*. Oxford: Oxford University Press.

Cartwright, N. 1989. *Nature's Capacities and their Measurement*. Oxford: Oxford University Press.

Chalmers, A. F. 1987. "Bhaskar, Cartwright and Realism in Physics", *Methodology in Science* 20, pp. 77–96.

D'Alembert, J. le R. 1743. Extract from *Traité de Dynamique*, translated by W. F. Magie, in *A Source Book in Physics*, W. F. Magie (ed.), pp. 55–8. New York and London: McGraw-Hill Book Company (1935).

Dennett, D. C. 1995. *Darwin's Dangerous Idea: Evolution and the Meanings of Life*. Harmondsworth: Penguin.
Dretske, F. I. 1977. "Laws of Nature", *Philosophy of Science* **44**, pp. 248–68.
Duhem, P. 1954. *The Aim and Structure of Physical Theory*, P. P. Wiener (trans.), translated from 1914 French edition. Princeton: Princeton University Press.
Elder, C. L. 1992. "An Epistemological Defense of Realism about Necessity", *The Philosophical Quarterly* **42**, pp. 317–36.
Elder, C. L. 1994a. "Higher and Lower Essential Natures", *American Philosophical Quarterly* **31**, pp. 255–65.
Elder, C. L. 1994b. "Laws, Natures and Contingent Necessities", *Philosophy and Phenomenological Research* **54**, pp. 649–67.
Ellis, B. D. 1965. "A Vindication of Scientific Inductive Practices", *American Philosophical Quarterly* **2**, pp. 296–305.
Ellis, B. D. 1979. *Rational Belief Systems*. Oxford: Blackwell.
Ellis, B. D. 1990. *Truth and Objectivity*. Oxford: Blackwell.
Ellis, B. D. 1996. "Natural Kinds and Natural Kind Reasoning", in *Natural Kinds, Laws of Nature and Scientific Methodology*, P. J. Riggs (ed.), pp. 11–28. Dordrecht: Kluwer Academic Publishers.
Ellis, B. D. 2001. *Scientific Essentialism*. Cambridge: Cambridge University Press.
Ellis, B. D. and Lierse, C. E. 1994. "Dispositional Essentialism", *Autralasian Journal of Philosophy* **72**, pp. 27–45.
Fales, E. 1990. *Causation and Universals*. London: Routledge and Kegan Paul.
Forster, M. R. 1988. "Unification, Explanation, and the Composition of Causes in Newtonian Mechanics", *Studies in the History and Philosophy of Science* **19**, pp. 55–101.
Galilei, G. 1623. "The Assayer", in *Discoveries and Opinions of Galileo*, S. Drake (ed. and trans.). New York: Doubleday Anchor Books (1957).
Goodman, N. 1955. *Fact, Fiction and Forecast*. Cambridge, Mass.: Harvard University Press.
Hall, A. R. 1954. *The Scientific Revolution 1500–1800*. London: Longmans Green.
Harré, R. and Madden, E. H. 1975. *Causal Powers: A Theory of Natural Necessity*. Oxford: Blackwell.
Hume, D. 1777. *Enquiries concerning Human Understanding and concernng the Principles of Morals*, 3rd edn, L. A. Selby-Bigge and P. H. Nidditch (eds). Oxford: The Clarendon Press (1975).
Iltis, C. 1973. "The Leibnizian–Newtonian Debates: Natural Philosophy and Social Psychology", *The British Journal for the History of Science* **6**, pp. 343–77.
Kant, I. 1787. *Critique of Pure Reason*, N. Kemp Smith (trans.). London: Macmillan (1950).
Kornblith, H. 1993. *Inductive Inference and its Natural Ground*. Cambridge, Mass.: MIT Press.
Kripke, S. 1972. "Naming and Necessity", in *Semantics of Natural Language*, D. Davidson and G. Harman (eds), pp. 252–355. Dordrecht: Reidel.
Kripke, S. 1980. *Naming and Necessity* (a revised and enlarged version of Kripke (1972)). Oxford: Blackwell.
Lakatos, I. 1970. "Falsification and the Methodology of Scientific Research Programmes", in *Criticism and the Growth of Knowledge*, I. Lakatos and A. Musgrave (eds), pp. 91–196. Cambridge: Cambridge University Press.
Laudan, L. L. 1968. "The *Vis Viva* Controversy, a Postmortem", *Isis* **59**, pp. 131–43.

Lewis, D. K. 1986. *On the Plurality of Worlds*. Oxford: Blackwell.

Lierse, C. E. 1996. "The Jerrybuilt House of Humeanism', in P. J. Riggs (ed.) *Natural Kinds, Laws of Nature and Scientific Methodology*, pp. 29–48. Dordrecht: Kluwer Academic Publishers.

Locke, J. 1690. *An Essay Concerning Human Understanding*, P. H. Nidditch (ed.). Oxford: The Clarendon Press (1975).

Magie, W. F. 1935. *A Source Book in Physics*. New York and London: McGraw-Hill Book Company.

Martin, C. B. 1980. "Substance Substantiated", *Australasian Journal of Philosophy* 58, pp. 3–10.

Martin, C. B. 1984. "Anti-realism and the World's Undoing", *Pacific Philosophical Quarterly* 65, pp. 3–20.

Martin, C. B. 1993. "Powers for Realists", in *Ontology, Causality and Mind: Essays in Honour of D. M. Armstrong*, J. Bacon, K. K. Campbell and L. Reinhardt (eds), pp. 175–94. Cambridge: Cambridge University Press.

Maxwell, N. 1968. "Can there be Necessary Connections between Successive Events?", *British Journal for the Philsosophy of Science* 19, pp. 1–25.

Mayer, J. R. 1842. "Remarks on the Forces of Inorganic Nature", G. C. Foster (trans.), in *A Source Book in Physics*, W. F. Magie (ed.), pp. 196–203. New York and London: McGraw-Hill Book Company (1935).

McCall, S. 1994. *A Model of the Universe*. Oxford: The Clarendon Press.

McCormmach, R. 1988. "Henry Cavendish on the Theory of Heat", *Isis* 79, pp. 37–67.

Nelson, A. 1990. "Are Economic Kinds Natural?" *Minnesota Studies in the Philosophy of Science* XIV, pp. 101–35.

Putnam, H. 1975. "The Meaning of 'Meaning'", *Minnesota Studies in the Philosophy of Science* VII, pp. 131–93.

Reichenbach, H. 1928. *The Philosophy of Space and Time,* Maria Reichenbach and John Freund (trans.). New York: Dover (1957).

Rosenberg, A. 1986. "Lakatosian Consolations for Economics", *Economics and Philosophy* 2, pp. 127–39.

Rosenberg, A. 1992. *Economics – Mathematical Politics or Science of Diminishing Returns*. Chicago, Ill.: University of Chicago Press.

Sankey, H. 1997. "Induction and Natural Kinds", *Principia* 1(2), pp. 235–54.

Sankey, H. (ed.) 1999. *Causation and Laws of Nature*. Dordrecht: Kluwer Academic Publishers, pp. 1–88.

Scriven, M. 1961. "The Key Property of Physical Laws – Inaccuracy", in *Current Issues in the Philosophy of Science*, H. Feigl & G. Maxwell (eds), pp. 91–104. New York: Holt Reinhart and Winston.

Sellars, W. 1963. *Science, Perception and Reality*. London: Routledge and Kegan Paul.

Shoemaker, S. 1980. "Causality and Properties", in *Time and Cause: Essays presented to Richard Taylor*, P. van Inwagen (ed.), pp. 109–35. Dordrecht: Reidel.

Shoemaker, S. 1983. "Properties, Causation and Projectibility", *Applications of Inductive Logic*, L. J. Cohen and M. Hesse (eds), pp. 291–312. Oxford: Oxford University Press.

Smart, J. J. C. 1993. "Laws of Nature as a Species of Regularities", in *Ontology, Causality and Mind: Essays in Honour of D. M. Armstrong*, J. Bacon, K. K. Campbell and L. Reinhardt (eds), pp. 152–69. Cambridge: Cambridge University Press. (Reply by D. M. Armstrong, pp. 169–74.)

Swinburne, R. 1983. "Reply to Shoemaker", in *Applications of Inductive Logic*, L. J.

Cohen and M. Hesse (eds), pp. 313–20. Oxford: Oxford University Press.

Swoyer, C. 1982. "The Nature of Natural Laws", *Australasian Journal of Philosophy* **60**, pp. 203–23.

Thayer, H. S. 1953. *Newton's Philosophy of Nature*. New York: Hafner Publishing Company.

Tooley, M. 1977. "The Nature of Laws", *Canadian Journal of Philosophy* 7, pp. 667–98.

van Fraassen, B. C. 1980. *The Scientific Image*. Oxford: The Clarendon Press.

van Fraassen, B. C. 1989. *Laws and Symmetry*. Oxford: The Clarendon Press.

Walras, L. 1874. *Elements of Pure Economics*, W. Jaffe (trans.). Homewood, Ill.: Irwin (1954).

Wilkerson, T. E. 1995. *Natural Kinds*. Aldershot: Ashgate Publishing Company.

Index

a priori knowledge, distinguished from a
    posteriori 17n
accidental properties, distinguished from
    essential 11
agency 141–4
    human 143–4,
    in nature 142–3
aim of science 115–18
analysis *see* logical analysis; realistic
    analysis.
analyticity 110–11, *see also* necessity
aposteriority 106–108
apriority, criteria of necessity and strict
    universality 106–109
Armstrong, David M. 7, 98, 167–71,
    171–2, *see also* Meinongian
    properties; Swinburne's regress

Bealer, George 7
Berkeley, George 22
Bhaskar, Roy 7, 94n, 160
Bigelow, John C. 7, 133
biological species, as cluster concepts 12,
    28–32, 154–7
Burtt, E. A. 60

Campbell, Keith K. 58
capacities 65–6, *see also* dispositional
    properties.
Carroll, John W. 7
Cartwright, Nancy 7

categorical properties 68–70, 173–6
    and causal powers 173–6
    nature of 68–70
categorical realism 70–6
    continuing existence argument for
        73–4
    critique of 73–6
    difference argument for 74
causal interactions 83–4
causal laws *see* laws of nature
causal powers 48–50
    active and passive 61–2
    Hume's theory of 48–50, 103–105
    meta- 31, 143–4
    objective 49
    as relations to natural kinds of
        processes 68
    as truthmakers for causal laws 102
causation
    essentialist theory of 50
    Hume's theory of 48–50
causes in Aristotelian metaphysics 9–
    12
    final 11–12, 13
Cavendish, Sir Henry 151
classifications 39
    based on intrinsic properties 40
    objective or mind-independent 40
conditionals
    assertibility conditions 134
    counterfactual or subjunctive 79

realistic analysis of truth conditions
for 131–3
conservation laws *see* laws of nature,
global.
contingency thesis 71–2
continuing existence argument *see*
categorical realism
conventionalist theory of laws 95–7
counterfactual conditionals *see*
conditionals, counterfactual.

d'Alembert, J. le R. 149–50n
Dennett, Dan 19n, 156
Descartes, René 2, 35, 60
dispositional properties 76–9
causal and stochastic 78
as grounds for natural kinds of
processes 77–8
as genuine properties 78–9
superiority of realistic analysis of 79
dispositional realism 70–6
argument from laws of nature for 75
argument from science for 74–5
contrasted with categorical realism
70–6
ontological argument for 76
dispositions 65–8
realistic analysis of 76–9
Dretske, Fred I. 7, 98
Duhem, Pierre 21, 22, 24, 32
dynamic universals *see* universals

economic essentialism 162–5
economics
as a pure science 148, 163–4
contrasted with physical theory 163–
5
Lakatosian methodology in 162
Elder, Crawford 7
empiricism 21–3
energy transfer processes 83–4
essences
Aristotelian 12
individual 12
Lockean 55–6
of natural kinds 12
real 54–6
real distinguished from nominal 16
essentialism

Aristotelian 9–12
in biology 11, 154–7
in economics 147–8
modern 12–19, 59–60
in the philosophy of mind 139–44
in physics 149–54
in social theory 145–7, 157–9
essentialist
explanations 159–61
theories of laws 100–102
Euler, Leonhard 62
events, necessary connections between
59, 72, 104, 110, 112
events and processes *see* natural kinds
explanations 21–5, 159–61
dispositional 77
essentialist 159–61
model theoretic 21–3, 53–4
causal process 23–5, 89
explanatory frameworks 24–5, 32
extensionality, requirement of in logical
analysis 128

Fales, Evan 7, 93n
forces
as external to objects 3, 63–5, 149–
51
Leibnizian and Newtonian concepts
of 149–52
Mayer's concept of 151–2
Forster, Malcolm 78
Frege, Gottlob 108

generic natural kinds *see* natural kinds
genidentity 30, 154–7
global laws *see* laws of nature, global
Goodman, Nelson 137

Hall, A. R. 81
Harré, Rom 7
Heil, John 7
Hilbert, David 108
Hume, David 2, 22, 48–9, 103–4, 111–
12
Hume worlds 175
Humean supervenience thesis 115–8
Humeanism 71, 114–17, 123–5
approximation defence of 93–4
common theses of 59–60

realistic analysis, programme of 126,
137–8
reality, Maxwell's criterion 25
Reichenbach, Hans 163
regularity theory of laws 72, 92–5
approximation defence of 93–4
relations *see* properties: properties and
relations are discussed together as
species of property universals
research programmes, hard core
assumptions and protective belts in
160–61
Russell, Bertrand 58, 127

Scriven, Michael 91n
semantics
of dispositional terms 76–9
modal 126–7, 130–2
"possible worlds" 117, 131–2
see also realistic analysis
sets, representation of properties as
128–30
Shoemaker, Sydney 7, 169
Smart, J. J. C. 25, 130
substances, not property instances 45–6
substantive universals *see* universals
supervenience *see* Humean
supervenience
Swinburne, Richard 169
Swinburne's regress 169, 171–2
Swoyer, Chris 7

theories
abstract model 21–3
causal process 23–5
Tooley, Michael 7, 98
tropes *see* properties
Twin Earth 16, 113

universal propositions, accidental and
nomic 88–92
universals (in ontology) 43, 67–8, 89,
97–9, 100–102, 176
accidental 89
generic 176
natural kinds as 100–102, 176
relations of natural necessitation
between 97–9

vacuous truth 15n
Van Fraassen, B. C. 90
vis viva controversy 149–52

Walras, Leon 148, 163
Wittgenstein, Ludwig 58
world
as one of a kind 118–20
natural necessities, possibilities and
contingencies in the 120
-objects 86–7
-processes 86
-properties 87–8
structure of the 118–19
see also Hume worlds; possible worlds